MW00477939

The Eightfold Path

Edited by Jikyo Cheryl Wolfer

Introduction by Byakuren Judith Ragir

with

Myoan Grace Schireson, Zenki Mary Mocine,
Tonen O'Connor, Shodo Spring, Misha Shungen Merrill,
Teijo Munnich, Hoko Karnegis, Pat Enkyo O'Hara

Temple Ground Press

Temple Ground Press
3248 39th Way NE
Olympia, WA 98506

Cover and interior design by Fletcher Ward.
Cover photograph by Jikyo Cheryl Wolfer.

Set in Adobe Garamond Pro 8/16.

ISBN 978-0985565152

Temple Ground Press, Olympia, WA

Dedicated to

Katsuryu Tetsumei Niho Roshi

Transmitter of the Dharma to America

on the occasion of his 77th year

with deepest gratitude for

the gift of his life.

Table of Contents

Preface

This book is the third in a series of Buddhist teaching anthologies offered by Soto Zen women and by Temple Ground Press. Previous anthologies published by Temple Ground are *Receiving the Marrow: Teachings on Dogen by Soto Zen Women Priests* (2012) and *Seeds of Virtue, Seeds of Change: A Collection of Zen Teachings* (2014). The impetus for Temple Ground Press originated several years ago during a conference dinner conversation among women Soto Zen priests. Temple Ground exists solely to bring forward Soto Zen women's voices within the book-publishing world, to bring to light the wisdom of teachers who might not otherwise be recognized, and to create future opportunities for these women to publish. In her introduction to *Receiving the Marrow*, editor and publisher Eido Frances Carney writes:

> Our concern in publishing women's voices is so future Zen students may be able to trace the history and articulation of women teachers of this century. . . . Since we ourselves are disappointed by limited evidence in researching our own lost sisters, we feel an obligation to care for the future by offering our voices now so we do not create an absence on which future claims of exclusion may be based. . . . In the history of the world's religions, we have a mere cupful of spiritual texts written by, or about women. (viii-ix)

Zen and Buddhism are uniquely positioned to remedy this silencing. The founder of Soto Zen, Eihei Dogen (Dogen Zenji, 1200-1253), spoke out strongly in favor of women and tells stories about several women Zen masters in his *Shobogenzo* fascicle "*Raihai Tokusui* (Respectful Bowing Will Secure the Very Marrow of the Way)." Dogen says, "Why should only males be worthy of respect? Boundless space is simply boundless space; the four elements are simply the four elements; the five skandhas are simply the five skandhas. And they are no different for women. When it comes to realizing the Way, everyone may realize It (Nearman 96)." Myoan Grace Schireson examines this history more closely in her book *Zen Women: Beyond Tea Ladies, Iron Maidens and Macho Masters* (Wisdom

2009), for even though Dogen spoke forcefully for women, actual practice in Japanese Zen temples in his time continued to support cultural rather than Buddhist traditions. Even today, women are not allowed to train as monastics in Dogen's own temple, Eiheiji. This custom limits their ability to become a part of or significantly influence the upper reaches of Soto Zen hierarchy.

One of my assignments as a graduate student in counseling psychology involved reading the text *Women's Ways of Knowing: The Development of Self, Voice and Mind*, a long-term study of women's unique ways of constructing knowledge. Reading this book, I felt validated for the first time for my unique way of knowing, which until that moment had often been criticized as "illogical." In this text, the French feminist Marguerite Duras is quoted as saying:

> Women have been in darkness for centuries. They don't know themselves. Or only poorly. And when women write, they translate this darkness. Men don't translate. They begin from a theoretical platform that is already in place, already elaborated. The writing of women is really translated from the unknown, like a new way of communicating, rather than an already formed language. (203)

Women's Ways was collaboratively written and presents the researcher's conclusions that women tend to rely more often on intuitive and experiential knowing rather than linear, structured intellectual knowledge and prefer working in relational collaboration as opposed to rigid hierarchical structures. Women's ways of knowing work well in Zen practice which advocates going beyond thought to the "unknowing" of mind-to-mind transmission. Women now comprise over half of the practicing Soto Zen Dharma teachers and temple founders. They have served or are serving as abbesses for large institutions such as San Francisco Zen Center, Los Angeles Zen Center, and Shasta Abbey. A lineage of Buddhist women, researched and created by women Zen priests, is now often provided at ordination along with, or incorporated into, the traditional male lineage chart. As women continue to suffer inequality and violence around the world and fail to penetrate the glass ceilings of many other spiritual hierarchies, Zen women priests are important examples of what is possible when the Buddha's principles of the equality and interdependence of all beings are actualized.

However, even in the world of Soto Zen, cultural factors still disadvantage women in some instances. True progress will have been made when a woman priest is elevated to the post of Soto Zen bishop for North America. I believe that day is coming.

The Buddha's foundational teaching of the Eightfold Path delineates the fundamental guidelines for anyone who contemplates embarking on a pilgrimage of the Buddha Way, or indeed, any spiritual path. It provides a trailhead, a starting point, from which to engage the practice of the Buddha's teachings, for the Buddha Way is a practice, not a set of prescriptions. As such, it must be actualized with the body and mind in this moment to be fully "known." In his commentary on *The Heart Sutra*, Red Pine, speaking of the early Buddhists, says, "[T]he Buddha's teachings were referred to as a system of training. . . . Thus, Buddhism is better understood as a skill or an art to be practiced and perfected rather than as information or knowledge to be learned and amassed (50)." Simply reading a description of the path will not provide that experience. To internalize and embody the Dharma, the teachings must be put into practice in this world of dissatisfaction.

In these pages, you will find maps and equipment for the pilgrimage. These teachings highlight the inherent uncertainty of following a path with no destination where no clear signage exists, where the landscape shifts in every moment, and where every step involves examination of intentions, motivations, and possible outcomes. They also emphasize how misunderstandings can arise when Buddhist practices, such as mindfulness, are separated from traditional understandings of these practices. The pilgrim never journeys alone, but is embraced by the Three Treasures—Buddha, Dharma, and Sangha—that function as a compass to keep the pilgrim's feet on the path; still the traveller is solely responsible to take compass readings at regular intervals.

It may be useful to note that varying translations exist for the names of the limbs of the Eightfold Path. Any choice of term must necessarily be arbitrary according to one's understanding and according to the aspect of Buddhist practice one wishes to emphasize. Zen teaches that language is unreliable and, at best, provides only an approximation of "true reality." To even label such a concept as "true" or "false" is a mistake. Nevertheless, each author provides us with a translation of their particular title that lifts the reader out of the cultural understanding of the English words and inspires insight into actions that support the practice of that limb of the Path.

Byakuren Judith Ragir introduces the Four Noble Truths and provides a useful map of the fourth Noble Truth, the Eightfold Path, from which to launch a deeper investigation of each limb. Myoan Grace Schireson explains how to invoke Right View and hone it with concentration practice; Zenki Mary Mocine explores the practices of renunciation, loving-kindness, and compassion as the underpinnings of Right Intention; Tonen O'Connor excavates the nuances of the Buddha's teaching on Right Speech. In this age of fragmentation, Shodo Spring issues an inspiring call to Right Action on behalf of the tribe of all beings, and Misha Shungen Merrill raises difficult questions for modern Buddhists in her thoughts about Right Livelihood. Teijo Munnich takes an unusual perspective on Right Effort as she contemplates the effects of profound grief; Hoko Karnegis masterfully unfolds Dogen's teachings on Right Mindfulness; and Pat Enkyo O'Hara introduces the Samadhi family. In every chapter, you will find instructions for various practices to use in daily life as well as to unerringly guide you along the Buddha Way.

For readers who may not be acquainted with Soto Zen, Eihei Dogen is the founder of Soto Zen in Japan, highly revered for his unique approach to Buddhist practice as well as for his consummate skill with language and extensive knowledge of Buddhism and Buddhist literature. These are demonstrated most thoroughly in his masterwork, *Shobogenzo* (The Treasury of the True Dharma Eye). These teachings consist of ninety-six chapters (fascicles) written over the course of Dogen's lifetime. He intended for the completed work to include one hundred chapters, but died before he could achieve that aim. This writing is arguably his most cited work as it is the seminal document for Soto Zen study. Dogen also wrote at length about practice rules for his monastic community (*Eihei Shingi*). His talks, koan commentaries, and poetry are collected in *Eihei Koroku* (Dogen's Extensive Record). This trinity of writings constitutes the foundational teachings of Soto Zen. A brief biography of Dogen can be found in *Receiving the Marrow* (xvii-xxix).

Preface

Editing an anthology is always a gift for which I am truly grateful: first, to my teacher, Eido Frances Carney, for her incomparable vision in founding Temple Ground Press; second, to each writer for her purposeful efforts, her profound teachings, and the gift of her life to the Dharma. Each new volume is a rich feast of varying dishes that allows me the privilege of ingesting the Dharma—chewing it, revisiting it, re-viewing it, fueling my spiritual growth. A common theme may thread through this book, but each writer's approach to Zen practice is unique. Their voices rise clearly from these pages.

Gratitude must also be extended to the cadre of Buddhist translators whose works are cited frequently within this volume. The realm of Buddhist textual translation and publishing is almost exclusively male, so we have managed to include male voices in this anthology after all. One cannot accomplish any task without the efforts of all beings. Some women translators are beginning to come forward, most recently Tonen O'Connor with her translation of Kodo Sawaki's *Commentary on the Song of Awakening* (U of Hawai'i, 2015). I personally hope more women Zen students and priests will accept the challenge of a life of translation and that our current translators will seek to mentor women Buddhists in this endeavor. We can never have too many translators; so many treasures remain to be interpreted, enough to encompass many lifetimes.

Further thanks go to Fletcher Ward, ancient dharma brother and founder of Straight Light Studio, whose patience is inexhaustible and whose creativity shines on every page of this book; to the long-suffering sangha at Joyous Refuge who have patiently endured a certain neglect during my labors; and to the suffering world that provides each being with the opportunity to encounter and practice the Dharma and to awaken. May all beings benefit from this offering.

Jikyo Cheryl Wolfer
Port Angeles, WA
June, 2016

Works cited

Belenky, Mary, Blythe Clinchy, Nancy Goldberger and Jill Tarule. *Women's Ways of Knowing: The Development of Self, Voice, and Mind.* 10th ann. ed. New York: Basic Books, 1997.

Carney, Eido Frances, ed. *Receiving the Marrow: Teachings on Dogen by Soto Zen Women Priests.* Olympia, WA: Temple Ground, 2012.

Dogen, Eihei. "On Respectful Bowing Will Secure the Very Marrow of the Way." *Shobogenzo: The Treasure House of the Eye of the True Teaching.* Hubert Nearman, trans. Mt. Shasta, CA: Shasta Abbey Press, 2007.

Pine, Red. *The Heart Sutra: The Womb of Buddhas.* Washington, D.C.: Shoemaker & Hoard, 2004.

The Four Noble Truths

Byakuren Judith Ragir

As a newcomer, I sat in a five a.m. meditation and watched the day being born. It was 1973. In the dark, I had ridden my bicycle over the Mississippi River Bridge to a section of town called Dinkytown near the University. There, in the second floor of a duplex, was a zendo in the living room where the small community sat in the early mornings. I sat down, cross-legged on a zafu. I heard silence and then the first birds singing. I saw the black night turn to grey to silver to a light yellow. My heart and mind opened to the wonders of the day. The power of that first morning meditation still motivates me. It was my first message of hope in a dreary and painful childhood.

Meeting Katagiri Roshi was a radical pivot point in my life, turning me away from "wanting to die" and towards "learning how to live." He often did that to me. Turned me around and pushed me back into my life.

My first private meeting with Katagiri Roshi was in a small, darkened room during a sesshin, a Zen seven-day meditation retreat. He seemed very exotic to me. A short Japanese man in his 40's wearing the full regalia of the Buddha's robes and shaved head. He spoke in a sweet incomprehensible English. I entered my first one-on-one meeting with Roshi, my heart pounding out of my chest and my adrenaline rushing through my veins. I made my three bows in the formal ritual and sat down. We sat in silence with his famous grimace of a smile. Maybe I could call it a half-frown as opposed to Thich Nhat Hanh's half-smile. I was very intimidated. He leaned over and said, "You can't escape pain!" and then rang the bell, which was an indication that the meeting was over and I should leave. Shocked, I left the room.

"But, but, but," I thought. Didn't the Buddha say?

> I teach one thing and one thing only: that is, suffering and the end of suffering.

Where was the teaching on the end of suffering? That's what I wanted to know. For the next two decades, I misunderstood Buddhism. Searching in the opposite direction of my teacher's words, I tried to transcend my human suffering. Now, after more than forty years, I'm much clearer. Trying to transcend human suffering doesn't work. The three poisons—greed, anger and ignorance—arise endlessly. The pain of this truth is called the First Noble Truth. Human suffering is a Holy Truth! Spirituality is not the way out; it is the way in.

THE BUDDHA'S FIRST DISCOURSE

The Four Noble Truths teaching is believed to be the Buddha's first discourse. After Siddhartha Gautama (the Buddha's family name) left the palace and his secular life, his intention was to achieve a spiritual breakthrough. His first teachers were the Hindu and Brahmin teachers of his time. He did many years of ascetic practices. He lived in the forest; he barely ate. He had a very strenuous religious discipline. At one of the turning points in his religious life, he appeared to be starving almost to the point of death. There are very alarming statues and drawings of an emaciated, skeleton-like Buddha. His ribs are totally exposed and he has no body fat at all. At this pivotal point, Siddhartha decided that the way of the ascetics was not working for him. He was no closer to enlightenment than before and he decided to change his practice. The Middle Way was born.

The Story of the First Discourse
From the *Dhammacakkappavattana Sutta*

The Buddha said, "It is not easy to attain enlightened happiness, with a body so excessively emaciated." And so he ate some boiled rice and porridge. When he ate this, the five monks who were practicing with him were disgusted and left him, thinking: "The ascetic Gotama now lives luxuriously; he has given up his striving and reverted to luxury." But the Buddha did not give up. He sat under the Bodhi tree with the commitment that he would sit until he understood and could verify the truth about human life.

After his experience meditating under the Bodhi tree, during which time he wrestled with Mara, the embodiment of human temptations, he saw the morning star and saw the truth of life with clarity. Afterwards, he decided that there was no way he could teach what he had learned because it was too subtle and unattainable by mere reasoning. No one would get it. If it was not understandable by thinking, he concluded that no one would believe him. As soon as the Buddha's thought reached the mythological realms, very quickly and spontaneously the Brahma Sahampati, the most senior of the Maha deities, became very concerned for the world. He appeared before the Buddha and encouraged the Buddha to teach. Brahma Sahampati said to the Buddha, "Venerable sir, let the Blessed One teach the Dhamma, let the Sublime One teach the Dhamma. There are beings with little dust in their eyes who are perishing through not hearing the Dhamma. There will be those who will understand the Dhamma." On hearing this, the Buddha changed his mind and began his search for someone to teach.

The Buddha thought about this: "To whom should I first teach the Dhamma? Who will understand this Dhamma quickly?" It then occurred to the Buddha that Alara Kalama, one of his previous teachers, could understand. The deities heard this and approached the Buddha and said, "Alara Kalama died seven days ago." Oh, what a loss, the Buddha thought. Contemplating again, "Who could understand?" the Buddha thought of Uddaka Ramaputta, another former teacher, but the deities told him that Uddaka Ramaputta had died during the night. Strange. The Buddha thought again and then he thought perhaps the five ascetics—the five monks whom he had practiced austerities with prior to his turn-around—could probably hear his new teaching and so, he set out for Varanasi in the Deer Park at Isipatana.

He met Ajivaka Upaka, called the naked ascetic, on the road between Gaya and Bodhi. Even though he gave a teaching to him, Ajivaka Upaka shook his head and turned away and departed.

He continued on and finally the Buddha saw that he was approaching the five monks. The monks saw him coming and agreed among themselves: "Friends, here comes the ascetic Gotama who lives luxuriously, who gave up his striving and reverted to luxury. We should not pay homage to him or rise up for him or receive his bowl and outer robe. But a seat may be prepared for him. If he likes, he may sit down."

However, as he approached, they found that they could not keep up their pact. One took his bowl and outer robe, another prepared a seat, and another set out water for his feet. And they called the Buddha, "friend."

The Buddha said, "You can't call me "friend" because I am the Tathagata and have attained the Truth. Monks, do not address the Tathagata by name and as "friend." I shall teach you the Dhamma. The Tathagata has not reverted to luxury nor has he given up his striving. The Tathagata has achieved the enlightenment and can teach you and practice with you."

And so, the five monks and the Tathagata began to live together: living simply, begging for food, and listening to the teaching. Soon, as the story goes, the five monks achieved an unshakable liberation. (Bodhi 64, 69-75)

This teaching to the five monks is called the first discourse or the Four Noble Truths.

In this first discourse, the Buddha corrected what he called "the Two Extremes." The first extreme is to pursue happiness through sensual pleasures without thought of any spiritual discipline. The second extreme is to have a severe sense of discipline, which may lead to self-mortification. The Buddha said both of these extremes did not lead him to enlightenment. Then he began to teach the Middle Way and to expound on the Four Noble Truths.

The Four Noble Truths

Effect	First Noble Truth	There is suffering in this world—*dukkha*. There is a constant stream of dissatisfaction in life.
Cause	Second Noble Truth	*Dukkha* is caused by our desires, attachments, clinging, or thirsting.
Effect	Third Noble Truth	Our personal desire system can be stopped or cessated. There is well-being and we can enjoy it. There is liberation.
Cause	Fourth Noble Truth	The Eightfold Path is the teaching, activity, and process of stopping our attachment to desires, which cause our suffering. This process can bring us freedom.

The chart above and the Four Noble Truths are based on the most basic principle in Buddhism, that of "cause and effect." The Truths are based on two sets of cause and effect. The First and Third Truths are effects caused by the Second and Fourth Noble Truths. Inherent in the principle of cause and effect is the great ability to change or transform. If you change the conditions that are the cause, the effects change. But we can misunderstand this by thinking too linearly. There is a great deal of mystery in the multi-dimensional process of *karma* or cause and effect. We can never understand fully or rationally the process of cause and effect. Many different times and dimensions play into its unfolding, and yet, we can trust in this ancient and recurring principle—the interdependence of all things. One condition always influences another.

The Four Noble Truths illustrate the process of freeing ourselves and becoming liberated. What is it that we have to do in order to get the results we want—well-being and freedom?

Because Buddhism in the beginning was an oral tradition, we have many numbered teachings. This system helped people memorize the teachings without aid of written material. I actually still find them helpful and have come to enjoy the numbers. Numbering is a quick way, what we might call a "sound bite," to remember the teachings.

For example, there are three phases to each Truth as written in the Pali Canon. The first phase is to recognize and have the knowledge of each truth. The second phase is to know the "tasks" that are to be achieved regarding each truth. These tasks of the second phase are:

1. To fully understand the truth;
2. To abandon what needs to be let go of;
3. To realize or actualize the truth; and
4. To develop and practice each truth continually.

In the third phase, a practitioner has fully developed and completed each of the previous tasks. This is to have a fully realized enlightenment.

The First Noble Truth
There is suffering in human life.

My teacher's first teaching to me, "You can't escape pain," is a bitter pill. It is not what we want to hear. Many of us hope that a spiritual life will eradicate our human suffering. In a way, it does, and in a way, it doesn't. What Buddhist practice does is change the way we view our suffering. If we hold our pain in a different way, we can actually change our whole perspective on life. That is the effect of applying the Four Noble Truths and engaging in Buddhist practice.

The First Noble Truth: There is suffering in this world, which Buddhists call *dukkha*. *Dukkha* doesn't really translate well as "suffering" or "pain." Sometimes the misunderstanding of *dukkha* has resulted in a misinterpretation of Buddhism as being nihilistic or negative. This misunderstanding says: "Life is pain." This is a very simplistic and inaccurate view of what the Buddha saw on his enlightenment night. *Dukkha* literally means: *Du*- "apart from" and *Kha* or *akash*, which translates as "space."

This translation implies the sense of being apart from the spacious, the perfect, and the complete. In this way, *dukkha* conveys the deepest anguish and dilemma of the "self." We interpret our "selves" in a state of separation from the whole. This sense of a separated "self" is the beginning of the misunderstanding of life. It's the beginning of our feelings of alienation and despair.

In another level of translation, *dukkha* actually comes from a Sanskrit word that refers to a wheel out of kilter. The out-of-true wheel creates constant hardship, just as a potter's wheel, when it is not centered, cannot make a true pot.

I often use the translation of *dukkha* as dissatisfaction. You could say that "dissatisfaction" comes about as the opposite of *sukha* (satisfaction), but that is a dualistic interpretation. If we are to use "dissatisfaction" as the translation of *dukkha*, it has to mean the suffering that comes both from dissatisfaction *and* satisfaction. Even when there is satisfaction or happiness or joy, that state can quickly turn into suffering if we think it is permanent. If we are wise, we can see that happiness comes and goes.

There is a continuum of pain, starting from small dissatisfactions to great pains of loss, failure, sickness, and death. Observing myself, it is quite shocking to see all the small never-ending dissatisfactions. For example, the first hour of my day may run like this: The alarm clock is too loud and I want to sleep longer. Out from the covers, it's too cold. The bathroom is dirty and disorganized. Where's the toothpaste? It's not where I left it. On and on *ad nauseum*. This is the way the human mind works without training. The underlying vibration of *dukkha* comes from the perpetual desire for our own personal pleasure in life. We pursue happiness in sensual pleasures. A child's voice within many of us says, "I want what I want and I want it now!"

The Buddha used a number, 83, which could be a 1000 or an infinite number, to quantify our human problems. These are the never-ending disappointments—the mind of complaint. Here is a story from the Buddha about our problems in life:

> A farmer came to the Buddha and laid out all his problems. The farmer hoped the Buddha, as a wise man, would help him resolve some of his problems.
> The Buddha said, "I can't help you."
> The astonished man said, "What do you mean?"
> The Buddha said, "Everyone has problems, in fact everyone has got all eighty-three problems and there's nothing you can do about it. If you fix one problem, another will pop up. There's nothing you or I or anyone else can do about it."
> The man became furious, "I thought you were a great teacher," he shouted. "I thought you could help me. What good is your teaching then?"
> The Buddha said, "Well, maybe it will help you with the eighty-fourth problem?"
> "What's the eighty-fourth problem?"
> The Buddha said, "You don't want to have any problems."
> (Hagen 16-17)

This is our fantasy that a spiritual life can eradicate our suffering. Katagiri Roshi kept turning me around and pushing me back into my life. There is "No Escape" and yet, as we change how we perceive our life, we begin to understand that there is no solid "self." With this adjustment in thinking, our relationship to our human suffering does start to change. We begin to acquire what Katagiri Roshi called "spiritual stability"—a place in ourselves that is quiet, connected to everything, and beyond personal identity. This provides us with an inner strength and resilience to see the real truth of the world. As we find this place in ourselves, our obsession with our problems seems to calm down and we begin to practice with things "as they are."

In the *Dhammacakkappavattana Sutta*, the Buddha describes the Noble Truth of suffering as having its origins in the following:

1. Birth is suffering, aging is suffering, illness is suffering, death is suffering.

2. Union with what is displeasing is suffering.

3. Separation from what is pleasing is suffering.

4. Not getting what one wants is suffering.

5. The five aggregates subject to clinging is suffering.
   (Bodhi 76)

As we begin to work with what causes our suffering, we can find what releases our suffering. A most important phrase for me, which I received decades ago from Steven Levine's work is: *The pain, not my pain.*

This is a quick way to remember that everyone experiences what I'm experiencing in life. It is part of being human. We cannot escape old age, illness, and death. No one gets around those things. We must find a much deeper way to relate to human suffering. When I think that "the pain" is connected to all humans, it becomes a doorway for me to open to humanity. I am not better or worse; my pain is not better or worse. This is "the pain" of being alive in a human form.

As we practice receiving pain in this way, our life opens up to what is real in this very moment. This moment, whatever it contains, is reality itself. If this moment is painful, the embracing of this moment's pain is the most alive practice. It breaks open my defenses and allows me to receive life's energy, including pain's energy, as the Buddha.

I was shocked years ago when I first heard Pema Chodron's teaching that *unrequited love is the center of the world.* That seemed the opposite of what my hope wanted—to escape life's sorrow through spirituality. That "unrequitedness" is the truth that when we come from our personal desires, we are always dissatisfied. It's impossible to wrestle with life and get everything we want. What Buddhists call *samsara*, the wandering-in-circles world, is this endless round of thwarted desires. We and *samsara* are always broken at the core. This brokenness is not bad. To the contrary, our brokenness is what helps us see that we are more than a unit of "self." In our brokenness, we see the interdependence of life. The deeper mystery is beyond our satisfaction and pleasure. Pema Chodron has called this the "soft spot" that allows us to be open.

Learning how to stay with our negative emotions and not turn away from the moment is one of our essential practices. We need to stay with our "soft spot." Our meditation practice is the laboratory in which we discover and find out how to stay with our negative emotions. This is especially true of longer meditation retreats where, inevitably, we have to sit with pain—physical or emotional. How do you do it? What has to happen in your body, in your heart, and in your mind to accept this moment of suffering? As we learn acceptance in our meditation practice, we can begin to extend it into our life activities.

Pema Chodron suggests that we "teach ourselves the dharma." One way of doing this is to use specific phrases, often corresponding to the Four Divine Abodes (loving-kindness, compassion, joy and equanimity). These are also sound bites for a quick mindful remembrance of the teaching. I use them every day and will include other suggestions as we go along. The use of phrases is one way to digest the intellectual ideas in Buddhism into the practical, ordinary flow of your day.

May I be present and stay open to pain.

One of Pema Chodron's formulas for practicing with our negative emotions and the inevitable pain that arises, is to learn how to stay with and digest our difficulties: don't repress your emotions; don't act them out; drop the storyline; and stay, stay, stay with the underlying energy of the moment. (Chodron 2005, tape 2)

To stay with the energy of the suffering of life when it arises is to meet our pain. Each emotion, each bit of human suffering, is expressed as an energy in the present moment. If we can remain with that energy, we are receiving our life and being in the present moment. My suffering radically changes if I actualize this teaching in my day-to-day life. My heart opens. The practice of returning to the Now actually stabilizes me. Dwelling in the ever-present now, we find a different kind of space. This is a space of an open, non-suffering, peaceful and timeless place. This refuge has the effect of reducing our suffering.

May my pain turn into wisdom and compassion.
May sorrow show me the way to compassion.

There is a strong connection with radical acceptance of our suffering and the development of compassion. Here are quotes from my teachers that reinforce this teaching.

In *The Heart of Buddha's Teaching*, Thich Nhat Hanh writes: "Because there is suffering in your heart, it is possible for you to enter the Buddha's heart. Your suffering and my suffering are the basic condition for us to enter the Buddha's heart, and for the Buddha to enter our heart (3)."

In *Returning to Silence*, Katagiri Roshi writes:

> Suffering is not merely suffering as opposed to pleasure. **Suffering is a holy truth**; this means that it is one aspect of human life from which no one can escape. It is completely beyond what one likes or dislikes. You have to face it directly because your life is right in the midst of suffering. Directly facing the suffering "as it is," is to be free of the suffering. It is an opportunity to touch the core of human life. This is the total acceptance of suffering. [emphasis added] (30)

To have a conscious relationship with suffering is different than having an unconscious one. The First Noble Truth brings this conscious relationship to the foreground. We get to know *dukkha* by meeting the experience of human suffering directly and by not adding our mental stories with their attachments and aversions. There are many phrases that direct us towards this teaching.

May I fully face life and death, loss and sorrow.
May I accept my suffering, knowing that I am not my suffering.

And from Thich Nhat Hanh: "My dear suffering, I know you are there, I am here for you, and I will take care of you (Bodhipaksa, para 7)."

THE SECOND NOBLE TRUTH
We cling to a personal desire system.

The Second Noble Truth brings forth what causes our suffering. There have been many words that have been used in the translations: desire, clinging, grasping, attachment, craving, thirsting and so forth. Thich Nhat Hanh suggests that the use of only one word—for example, craving—is a misunderstanding of the sutra. He says that all the afflictions were written out as the cause of our suffering. Abbreviations are often used throughout the sutras. He suggests that only the first affliction—craving—was used as the abbreviated form of the entire list (Nhat Hahn 22). So the question becomes: What are the true afflictions that cause our suffering?

The nobility of the Second Truth comes from knowing we can't extinguish desire. Buddhism doesn't ignore desire or try to destroy it. We practice with it. Though our attachments cause our problems, we learn pivot around them and use our desires for the benefit of others and not only for ourselves.

Our desires come from holding on to that which we think will produce happiness for our self. Part of the work in Buddhism is the deconstruction of a solid sense of "self." We redirect ourselves to the teaching of interdependence, which makes our "selves" more porous. Otherwise, if we believe in this singular "self," we then have to defend it and try to grasp what the "self" thinks it needs. That is what I call a personal desire system—a system built around a "self" and its imagined needs.

The Buddha spoke about three hungers that help to produce this system of desires. These are the basic human instincts that create our complex arrangement of desires. The Three Hungers are:

1. Wanting to hold on to sensual pleasure;

2. Craving being, wanting to be alive; and

3. Craving non-being, wanting to escape the pain of being alive.

The first hunger is quite easy to understand. A desire to prolong sensual pleasure implies an aversion to pain and difficulty. We want sensual pleasure, friendships that are easy, and we do not want to face our difficulties.

The second hunger is the craving for being. Our most basic instinct is to physically survive. We honor birth and are afraid of death. In interpersonal relationship, we hunger to be seen, and we have a fear of invisibility (Kramer 34).

The third hunger is the craving for non-being. These are our urges to escape life and its problems. In a spiritual life, it is the craving for transcendence and an attachment to emptiness. In Zen, we sometimes call this "void sickness." This craving for oblivion is also the basis for the painful attraction to suicide. Interpersonally, we may be afraid of intimacy and relationship, and want to escape being seen (Ibid).

These hungers function within us all the time. To bring them into awareness helps us make our choices with more consciousness.

In addition to the Three Hungers, my clearest understanding of the Second Noble Truth comes through study of the Three Objects and Three Poisons. The sound bite for this teaching is from the Tibetan Lojong slogans:

Three objects, three poisons, and three seeds of virtue.
(Chodron 1994, 28)

The objects are our instinctual reactions to the outer environment. This reaction is biological. For example, an amoeba or a cell knows instinctively if it should take in, reject, or pass by different chemicals. However, the human consciousness elaborates on the object and includes it in a story about the "self." This neutral object then turns into one of the poisons: greed, anger and ignorance. These poisons create suffering in our world.

Three Objects	Three Poisons	Explanation of the Poisons
Like	Greed, passion	Attachment, desire, wanting, addiction to pleasure
Dislike	Anger, aggression	Aversion, violence, rage, hatred, irritation
Neutrality	Ignorance	Holding on to an idea of a self, which produces a personal desire system; living on automatic pilot; being in denial

As the chart suggests: "Liking" turns into clinging and attachment; "disliking" turns into aversion and hatred; "ignorance and not noticing" keeps the cycle of poisons arising endlessly.

The predicament of the objects and poisons is the field for our practice. We have the marvelous invitation to practice continuously because these poisons arise continuously. The second Bodhisattva Vow in the Zen tradition exemplifies this: "Greed, anger and ignorance arise endlessly, I vow to end them." In this same spirit is another Lojong slogan:

When the world is filled with evil,
transform all mishaps into the path of Bodhi. (Chodron 1994, 44)

The world is filled with poisons, which we can surely verify every morning by reading the newspaper. Our job as practitioners is to transform all the misfortunes that appear directly in front of us into the path of practice.

Another teaching that helps us understand attachment is the Eight Worldly Winds. These are the winds of the swirling world of our environment. As the winds of the outer world blow around us, how do we react to them? The Eight Worldly Winds are expressed as forms of duality.

The Eight Worldly Winds
Pleasure and Pain
Gain and Loss
Success and Failure
Praise and Blame

There are many translations of the Eight Worldly Winds but I adopted the wording above. We all want to attach to the side of pleasure, gain, success, and praise, and we fight to get rid of pain, loss, failure, and blame, but both the positive and the negative sides will inevitably arise. How can we welcome either side as Buddha itself, as the energy of the moment itself? This is the essential practice of non-reactivity. How do we stay centered in the face of the predictability of the Worldly Winds? Here is an equanimity phrase that helps me practice with these vicissitudes in life.

May I be at peace with the ups and downs of life.

Another question from the first Lojong slogan I mentioned is: What does it mean to plant "seeds of virtue"? Our practice is to bring forth a seed of virtue each time the poisons or the winds arise. These seeds can be as small as a mustard seed. They can be just a thought in the mind or a very small action. No matter how large or small, we plant a seed of virtue, right in the middle of our likes and dislikes. These seeds of virtue are any spiritual concept or quality that may help the situation, such as: kindness, patience, clarity, changing our habits, bringing forth a soft heart, reconnecting with universal energy, and opening up to something larger than our concept of a "self."

In the Zen vernacular, we have the wonderful teaching from Jianzhi Sengcan, the third Chinese ancestor of Zen, who lived primarily in the sixth century. In his poem *Trust in Mind*, he writes a very famous stanza:

The Great Way is not difficult
For those who have no preferences.
When love and hate are both absent
Everything becomes clear and undisguised. (Soeng 133)

Here, love and hate correspond to the poisons. When our attachments to the positive things of life and our aversion to the negative things are absent, life presents itself just "as it is" and each moment is "suchness" itself.

With this equanimity at the center of our life, we are not tossed away by outer circumstances. It is like the image of an Iron Man in Zen; the iron person can stay with his or her vows and spiritual principles through any swirling of the outer world. Our equanimity and compassion for life is unshakable.

"Iron" does not imply that we are stubborn and cold in the ordinary sense of the metal called "iron." In this metaphor, "iron" connotes an inner stability, equanimity, and wisdom. It is always there, completely reliable, resilient, and not affected by the Eight Worldly Winds. In the Buddhist way of thinking, if we have imperturbability at our core, our minds can be soft, flexible and compassionate with things "as they are."

THE THIRD NOBLE TRUTH
The personal desire system can be released.

The Third Noble Truth in Buddhism is the possibility of well-being and freedom. It is possible to heal our difficult lives. We can be restored to well-being. This well-being is the effect of practicing the Eightfold Path, the Fourth Noble Truth.

As we begin to soften our egocentric desires, our endless chasing after satisfaction will relax. Our natural wholeness is apparent as it is, always here and now. This is not something we attain. It is more an unraveling of our idea of a separate self. We can let go of the defenses that go along with protecting the "self." We have always been whole. This person right here has never been separated from the mystery of life. The experiencing of this truth creates a lessening of our suffering. We will have a greater ease with life. Our compassion will grow for the unending problems of being human.

From Katagiri Roshi's *Each Moment is the Universe*:

Just like everything that exists in the phenomenal world, your suffering is a being that arises from the original nature of existence,

14

and every moment it returns to its source. So when you see suffering, all you have to do is accept it and offer your body and mind to ultimate existence. Then you and suffering return to emptiness and there is freedom from suffering. (51)

It is not easy to let go of the way we have been brought up to see the world. We have to begin to see the world with different eyes—our buddha's eyes. What does Katagiri Roshi mean when he says "you offer your body and mind to ultimate existence"? That's a good koan question to contemplate. We can learn the art of stopping our old ways of seeing and our old habits. This new way of seeing helps us to go beyond conventional reality, which is based on appearance only. We can learn to "return to the source."

One of my teachers in the Tibetan tradition, Dan Brown, says that we must learn to live from a "different basis of operation." Even though the ordinary actions of life don't change, we learn to maintain a radically different view of what is actually happening through all of life's various conditions.

We also can learn to refrain from doing the things that cause us harm. Mindfulness is the energy that can help us stop. We can practice the cessation of our greed, anger and ignorance. Each moment can be seen as arising and returning to the Whole.

Enlightenment or cessation is not an "event" that happens in the future, and magically, our suffering is ended. The Buddha most often taught of a gradual cessation of hunger. The Eightfold Path is a process of becoming more and more immersed in practice. The "idea" that we practice now and later we are enlightened is also just one of our "ideas." If we truly deconstruct our ideas of time, we find that: Now is caused by our past, but the past doesn't actually exist; Now causes the future, but the future doesn't actually exist. This understanding of time helps us to see that the goal we want is just an idea we project into a future that doesn't exist. There is a Lojong slogan that examines this idea:

No hope for fruition. (Chodron 1994, 96)

There is no other place for enlightenment to happen than right now. Hoping for the fruition of our efforts in the future is not based on what is real—the future is an illusion. Our hope is a fantasy. With that in mind, ideas of gradual and sudden enlightenment seem kind of ridiculous. In the deepest sense, cause and effect arise together, all in the present moment.

Katagiri Roshi says:

> Zen is a practice of action. Sometimes people think that Zen practice is a bridge between suffering and happiness; we practice first and then we will be happy. But practice and happiness are not separate. Practice is not a bridge—practice itself is joy.
>
> Practicing egolessness doesn't mean that you destroy yourself and then something changes in the future. It means that egolessness comes up simultaneously with the activity of practice itself. The practice of subject and object merged into the present activity encourages us to let go of our interpretations. Grief becomes grief, loss becomes loss, and we have the comfort of holding them with universal perspective.
>
> This refined activity very naturally leads you to forget yourself.
> (2007, 125)

For me it is imperative that I not see egolessness as an encouragement to destroy myself or turn away from taking care of my karmic life. This is a very nihilistic and anti-life interpretation. Rather, these teachings are an encouragement to take care of our karmic life from a different vantage point, that of interdependence. There is a great sweetness in loving your life, accepting your life, and taking care of it from the eyes of a Buddha.

In order to understand this self-forgetting that Katagiri Roshi speaks of, it is very important to contemplate the most basic wisdom teachings. The three Dharma Seals are the basic teaching on the understanding of wisdom. (Nhat Hanh 122)

The first Dharma Seal is "impermanence." Life is a ceaseless coming and going, a constant flux and change. In physics we say there is literally nothing but motion. Scientists have found that there is no solid particle. With their sophisticated equipment, all the physicists find is space and energy. This corresponds in Buddhism to our understanding of no centralized self or no centralized "god." This constant flux is impermanence in Buddhism. Everything is moving but there is no solid particle. Nirvana is seeing thoroughly and completely that this is so.

Which leads to the second Dharma Seal—"non-self or no centralized self." A practitioner says "no" to a self that is permanent, unitary and independent. We say "yes" to inter-being and interdependence. The Buddha referred to what we call a person as simply a "stream" of different energies coming together.

The third Dharma Seal has an interesting development. Throughout my early study, I always learned that the third seal was the inevitability of *dukkha* (the First Noble Truth). But recently, both the Dalai Lama and Thich Nhat Hanh changed the name of this seal. Thich Nhat Hanh lists *nirvana* as the third seal (ibid). In his book *Essence of the Heart Sutra*, the Dalai Lama lists *dukkha* as the first seal and *nirvana* as the fourth seal (91-97). I interpret this arrangement as the human ability to transform *samsara* into *nirvana* through insight. When we open a seed of virtue or wisdom in each moment, we live in *nirvana*. Our practice becomes *nirvana* or, in other words, our practice becomes realization itself. Right in the place of holding on is the place of letting go.

Katagiri Roshi writes on cessation:

> In a moment you go beyond the phenomenal world of time and space to the source of time, where your life is calm and stable and your activity is clear and pure. When there is no self-consciousness it is called Bodhi, or enlightenment. Bodhi-mind is freedom. It is the function of mind that is beyond dualistic consciousness but to arouse bodhi-mind we have to use our discriminating human mind. In other words, the Buddha's mind is beyond human consciousness, but the only way to find out what it is, is through conscious activity. That is why we practice. (2007, 126)

Katagiri Roshi said that at the bottom of suffering, you will find emptiness. I add that at the bottom of your suffering is a door. That door opens, and you see Avalokiteshvara, the bodhisattva of compassion. Avalokiteshvara can embrace you, and then "you" can dissolve and become Avalokiteshvara yourself.

THE FOURTH NOBLE TRUTH
The Three Bases: Living the Eightfold Path to well-being.

The Eightfold Path, sometimes called the Eight Limbs, is the "how to" of the Buddha Way. It is a structure that encompasses the Buddhist teaching and how to practice with those teachings. It is the cause for the effect of the Third Noble Truth of liberation.

The core of the Eightfold Path is the Three Bases: wisdom (*prajna*), concentration (*samadhi*) and ethics (*sila*). The three bases are sometimes called the three-fold training. These bases are like a stool with three legs. All three legs of the stool have to be stable and strong for the stool to work as a seat. Our spiritual life is the same. In fact, I think the three bases is one of the most important teachings for twenty-first century Buddhism. If we understand the three bases, our practice will be integrated. Understanding and using the entirety of the Eightfold Path could correct many of the problems of unbalance in our sanghas and in our personal practices.

THE THREE BASES
and

The 8 limbs of the Eightfold Path

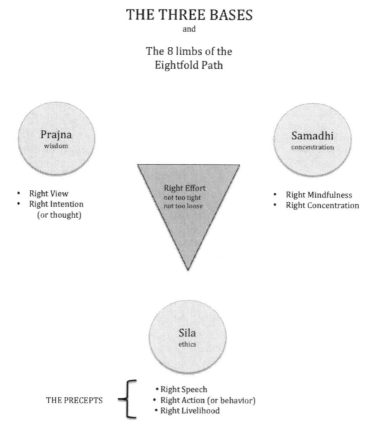

Prajna
wisdom

Samadhi
concentration

- Right View
- Right Intention
  (or thought)

Right Effort
not too tight
not too loose

- Right Mindfulness
- Right Concentration

Sila
ethics

THE PRECEPTS
- Right Speech
- Right Action (or behavior)
- Right Livelihood

I made this chart after many years of teaching, to help visualize our practice path and to help me memorize the Eightfold Path. Visually, I changed one thing from the original teaching, which is to put Right Effort in the center of the triangle. Right Effort would normally be under *samadhi* or concentration.

The teaching of the three bases helps me teach and practice in a manner that encourages spiritual integration. As we have seen historically, many teachers and sanghas have been severely damaged by adhering to a lopsided practice. Mostly, what I have experienced is ethical misconduct. When Thich Nhat Hanh came to America in the 1970s, he insisted that Americans needed to work with *sila* (ethics) to correct our imbalance. In my opinion, an understanding of the three-legged stool of training is the antidote to this lopsidedness.

Of what use is the achievement of *samadhis* and *jhanas* (meditative states), if they are not imbued with wisdom? How does wisdom serve us if it doesn't penetrate through to our behavior? The purpose of a spiritual life is to align our action with our understanding. Our ordinary actions in life must show substantial change, for the practice of Buddhism to be beneficial. We must become better human beings.

If we don't deepen our understanding through concentration and wisdom, Buddhism doesn't offer any real relief or freedom. When I observe the state of Buddhism in America today, I sometimes feel that we are losing depth. Buddhism does have tools that are needed by everyone and should be taught to everyone. Meditation and mindfulness can help everyone reduce suffering caused by our overwhelming modern stress, but there still must be a strain of practice that goes beyond stress-reduction. If we lose the existential aspect of Buddhism, we lose the real catalyst of our freedom. In the original teaching, the Buddha taught the three bases of training as the Way of liberation. The integration of all three bases is essential to a balanced practice, which is the true source of our release from the bondage of self and our ability to help others in the bodhisattva way of life.

To deepen our understanding of the Eightfold Path, we have to explore the word "Right." It is not "right" as opposed to "wrong" in a dualistic way of thinking. It is not good or bad, because there are no solid, unchanging definitions of good and bad. A famous Buddhist story illustrates the changing views of good and bad:

> In a village, a farmer's horse runs off. The villagers say, "Oh, too bad. You've lost your horse." A while later the horse comes back

accompanied by a herd of wild horses. The villagers say to the farmer, "Oh how lucky you are, you now have a herd of horses." The farmer's son then tries to ride one of the untamed horses and breaks his leg. The villagers say, "Oh, too bad, I'm so sorry." Next, the army comes to town, recruiting all the young men but the farmer's son is passed over because he has a broken leg! All the villagers say, "Oh what good luck you have." In the ever-changing circumstances of life, who knows what is good and what is bad? (Hagen 42)

This story encourages us to look deeper into what "right" means. The most literal translation of "right" is *samma* meaning: To go along with; to go together; to turn together; originally coming from the term that means "to unite."

This "uniting" is the meaning of "right." The interconnected Dharma is "right." This is a much larger understanding than right as opposed to wrong. Katagiri Roshi said: "Right activity is the actualization of the phenomenal world and the source of existence coming together and working together (2007, 126)."

There is a very famous Rumi poem that expresses this. The first lines of the poem are: "Out beyond ideas of wrongdoing and rightdoing, there is a field. I'll meet you there."

By placing Right Effort in the center of the stool, I am suggesting that Right Effort is necessary as the source point for all our practice and all the other bases. There are many words for effort—the energy of practice, diligence or determination in practice, enthusiasm, optimism or vigor. Right Effort is the Middle Way. Pema Chodron teaches a very useful phrase for Right Effort: *Not too tight, and not too loose.* I also like to use the phrase Right Amount in conjunction with Right Effort. What is the Right Amount of something that will produce well-being in others and ourselves?

The Eightfold Path opens with the Wisdom teachings of Right View and Right Intention, sometimes called Right Thought. Right View is the change of operation in our minds and perceptions that allows true understanding. Pema Chodron says it quite simply: "Wisdom is knowing what helps and what hurts." Right Intention comes out of our deep understanding of the Four Noble Truths. The content of our thoughts and our intentions directs our actions.

With the wise discernment of the first base of *prajna*, or wisdom, we can turn to our actions in life. *Sila*, or ethics, concerns itself with Right Speech, Right Behavior, sometimes called Right Action, and Right Livelihood. The precepts are deeply connected with this base. We learn how to behave like a Buddha in the world. The importance of our behavior is demonstrated in a deep way in Zen. Most Zen ceremonies are, in essence, an upholding of the precepts. The core teaching in each ceremony is the receiving of the precepts.

The last base is that of *samadhi* or concentration. It includes Right Meditation (or one-pointedness) and Right Mindfulness. Classically, Right Effort would be included in this base. Concentration is the ability to place our mind where we want it to be. We can hold our mind on one point—the aliveness of this very moment. Learning to concentrate the mind gives us the power to observe our actions and to make sure they align with our wise understanding.

Right Meditation is learning how to do zazen and how to increase our ability to receive the moment "as it is" in non-activity. Right Mindfulness is learning how to keep our mind on the present moment in activity. Both of these Limbs give us strength and steadfastness, deeply grounding all our action in "now."

If we have the steadfastness to remember the three bases, wisdom, ethics, and concentration, we can stop the swirling world of *samsara* and find the freedom that Buddhists talk about. Continuous practice becomes easier as our life becomes a series of moments. With this new outlook, suffering has a different feel to it. We can find the universal perspective in the particulars of our ordinary life and be free. We can move from a mind of complaint to a mind of gratitude. (Krech 13)

With this new perspective, we can receive and deeply feel the natural suffering that comes from being a human. The Holy Truth of suffering is practiced with grace. With this vastness in mind, we can begin to see the world as a field of action and service in which we can accomplish the Four Bodhisattva Vows.

> Beings are numberless; I vow to free them.
> Delusions are inexhaustible; I vow to end them.
> Dharma gates are boundless; I vow to enter them.
> The Buddha way is unsurpassable; I vow to realize it. (Sotoshu 74)

This is the way to end suffering. We don't annihilate our life and its particulars; we train ourselves to hold our life in the largest view possible. The Whole Dynamic Working of the Universe (*zenki*) helps us at every turn. We are at once completely ourselves and our life is completely its own life. Yet, simultaneously, we view our life from the vantage point of the Buddha's eyes.

Taken together, all aspects of the Eightfold Path teach us how to create a spiritual life. We can construct a balanced vehicle for practice/realization. For Buddhists, practice of the Eightfold Path is an examination of what it means to be a part of the Way.

As this book continues to elucidate the Path more specifically, each chapter, written by a different Zen teacher, unpacks and offers practices that promote understanding of a particular limb. Each limb has a long heritage of teaching, and if you study one limb, you can simultaneously experience them all.

One unique quality of this book is that women created it. When I go to the Soto Zen Buddhist Association conventions, about half of the teachers are now women. This influx of women's influence on Buddhism may be a leading component in the construction of American Buddhism in the twenty-first century. Let us continue to publish and see what the feminine perspective has to contribute.

Works cited

Bodhi, Bhikkhu, ed. "Dhammacakkappavattana Sutta, 5. The First Discourse." *In the Buddha's Words: An Anthology of Discourses from the Pali Canon.* Boston: Wisdom, 2005.

Bodhipaksa. " 'True Love: A Practice for Awakening the Heart' by Thich Nhat Hahn." *Wildmind Buddhist Meditation.* Wildmind, 2000-2015. Web. 3 May 2016. <www.wildmind.org/blog/bookreviews/true-love-thich-nhat-hanh>

Brown, Dan. "Lectures on Mahamudra." Mount Madonna Retreat Center, Watsonville, CA. February 2012.

Chodron, Pema. *Getting Unstuck; Breaking Your Habitual Patterns and Encountering Naked Reality.* Audiotapes. Sounds True: 2005.

---. *Start Where You Are*. Boston & London: Shambhala, 1994.

Dalai Lama. *Essence of the Heart Sutra*. Boston: Wisdom Publications, 2002.

Hagen, Steve. *Buddhism Plain and Simple*. New York: Broadway Books, 1997.

Katagiri, Dainin. "Thirsting Desire." *Returning to Silence*. Boston: Shambhala, 1988.

---. "Fundamental Suffering as Truth." and "The Practice of Creative Action." *Each Moment is the Universe*. Boston: Shambhala, 2007.

Kramer, Gregory. "The Second Noble Truth, Interpersonal Hunger." *Insight Dialogue, The Interpersonal Path to Freedom*. Boston: Shambhala, 2007.

Krech, Gregg. *Naikan, Gratitude, Grace, and the Japanese Art of Self-Reflection*. Berkeley, CA: Stone Bridge Press, 2002.

Nhat Hanh, Thich. *The Heart of the Buddha's Teaching: Transforming Suffering into Peace, Joy and Liberation*. Berkeley, CA: Parallax Press, 1998.

Salzberg, Sharon and Halifax, Joan. "Meditations and Four Divine Abode phrases." *Upaya Zen Center*. Upaya Zen Center, 2015. Web. <http://www.upaya.org/dox/meditations.pdf>.

Soeng, Mu. "Clarke Translation." *Trust in Mind, The Rebellion of Chinese Zen*. Boston: Wisdom, 2004.

Sotoshu Shumucho. *Soto School Scriptures For Daily Services and Practice*. Tokyo: Sotoshu Shumucho and the Soto Zen Text Project, 2001.

CHAPTER I

Right View and Its Actualization

Myoan Grace Schireson

The Buddhist Four Noble Truths are descriptive truths that define human life, suffering, and the cessation of suffering. These truths were the basis of the Buddha's teaching more than 2500 years ago as described in detail in the Introduction. The fact of suffering is the ground of Buddhist practice; the place of suffering is the human body; the cessation of suffering is the boundless sky—the vast expanse of freedom. The Four Noble Truths are conclusions about the nature of this human life; therefore, they are nouns—one of which, the Eightfold Path, is the solution to suffering. The Eightfold Path is the continuous activity of living on the ground while exploring the vast expansive sky.

The Eightfold Path is an ongoing experiential process, so following the Eightfold Path is not something you get or have, it's something you do. Even the use of the word "path" suggests movement; we may walk, we may continue along, and we may explore all of the possibilities we encounter along the way. We travel this path, we walk this path, and as Zen students, our life becomes a walking pilgrimage to practice. We consciously engage the eight limbs of this path because each limb integrates daily life activity. We remain on this path to grow and develop harmoniously with the Buddhist Way. Finding and adhering to this path requires Right View: realizing that Buddhism, rather than our current course of endless craving, can help end our suffering.

Watching life from Right View is also a continuous activity, not an object that we grasp and keep. Understanding Right View means to accept that the activity of practice, not impulse, will help us live more fully. We initiate Right View and learn to activate and stabilize Right View on the meditation cushion. The experience of Right View, the view from the cushion, becomes familiar to us; it is the view of this very moment as it is, not as we wish it to be. We strengthen Right View by returning to meditation. This act of returning to Right View is also a verb.

The entire Eightfold Path depends on Right View. Within Right View, we use all of the skills of the Eightfold Path to perceive and engage with the reality of this moment. From Right View, we can identify words and actions that help us to proceed from a practice perspective. Right View requires a shift from our habitual selfishness to a life-centered view. For example, if anger arises, we consider what is Right Speech or Right Action. We may slow down or refrain from an impulse to strike back. We may then proceed to Right Concentration to deepen the experience of practicing in everyday life.

Resting in Right View, we resist the aim to protect the imaginary self on its imaginary and proprietary cloud. Right View functions to help us see all of life as interconnected and unfolding in an unbounded sky. Encountered beings and claims arise and fall. As Uchiyama Roshi taught, "everything you encounter is your life (Uchiyama 39)." When your life includes everything, this is Right View. From this perspective, we rely on a stable faith in and experience of no abiding self, interconnectedness, and impermanence. By returning to these foundations of Right View, the mind becomes a cooking pot for the transformation of delusions, the release of attachments, and the basis for wholesome actions.

This is why Right View is the beginning, the middle, and the return to the Eightfold Path. It is only by means of Right View that we can identify the rest of the steps on the path of Buddhist practice. We need to be able to see, to feel, and to know when we are on the path, and when it is time to turn, go straight on, to stop, or to reverse direction. It is only from Right View that we can identify the time to strengthen Right Intention, to generate Right Speech and Right Action, to choose Right Livelihood, to practice Right Meditation and Right Concentration, and to enjoy Right Samadhi. How would we recognize the clarity or confusion in any situation if we had not activated Right View?

ACTIVATING RIGHT VIEW IN MEDITATION

In meditation, by intentionally bringing body, breath, and mind to one place, we begin to perceive true reality. We stop dreaming and scheming and begin to be more fully present. This is Right View. Again, finding Right View does not mean grasping or owning anything. It is better to think of Right View as Right *Viewing*. Finding Right View is an activity we engage in—or not. Engaging Right View plunks us smack down in the center of our own living reality. We turn away from the thinking-feeling-imagining function of our minds and toward our felt experience of the present moment.

Zen meditation is the activity of becoming the personal self, vividly illuminated through the view of oneness. When we practice meditation, we sit with this very personal body, experiencing the flow of the universal force. We can experience both unity and separateness as we view our relationship to oneness through our own body-mind equipment. It is on the meditation cushion that we may regularly access Right View, experiencing our personal mind and its activity within universal awareness.

However, Right View does not mean we just indulge in self-centeredness and discriminations or zone-out in the realm of Oneness. The ancient Buddhist text, *Sandokai: Merging of Difference and Unity* states: "Grasping things is basically delusion. Merging with principle is still not enlightenment (Okumura, 207)." Right View is neither grasping nor merging, nor is it alternating equally between the two actions. One observes simultaneously the attempts at grasping and the experience of merging. A Zen meditator experiences the mind's grasping while intimate with the absolute. This is how Right View functions.

In Zen meditation, the body and mind are the gate through which the entire universe moves. One breathes in the entire universe, one exhales to the farthest reaches of the universe. In his book, *Zen Mind, Beginner's Mind*, Suzuki Roshi described the self as the door that swings open and closed with each breath (29). But it is not "my" breath; it is the breath of the entire universe. This is the way Right View emerges on the meditation cushion. Each individual personally interacts with the entire universe. Wherever we are, our personal actions echo through the whole universe. To meditate is to enact and experience Right View.

We also continue to activate Right View off the cushion. Like a walking path we sense beneath our feet, we develop a stable, felt sense of Right View throughout a variety of meditation experiences. Whether we are at home or in a formal meditation retreat, we recognize what it feels like to find Right View. Finding Right View is what Eihei Dogen called "taking the backward step." While meditating, we step back from selfishness to spaciousness; then we return to daily activity with a spacious view that transcends our limited mind, even as we watch it.

Once we find Right View on the cushion, we may revisit it, but we don't own it. If you think about following a trail, you see it or feel it under your feet, but you may also make use of signposts or a map. Feeling Right View under your feet refers to finding the sense of spacious mind that orients away from selfishness to being present in this moment with life as it is. This is an open-sky mind; thoughts and impulses cross the sky like clouds, but the sky, not the clouds, defines the view.

We also find the path when we have stepped off of it. Strong sensations alert us to activate practice, just as bumpy rocks or brush remind us to pay more attention to the trail upon which we are walking. We look for the signposts of the path when we notice that our mind has gone astray. We note important landmarks on our practice path—decisions that either return us to our practice or distractions that take us far away from our intended route. Signposts may also include a sense of greater depth or ease of practice. These affirming indicators help to build confidence in the practice. If we stray, we can also find our way back to the path through the Dharma teachings. We use the teacher or the teaching words as a map to encourage us to return to practice. Sometimes these teachings help us find a direct route back to our path.

Within Right View one faces the trickery of persistent selfish impulses. Inhabiting and strengthening the stability of Right View, we have faith in the wholesomeness of Zen practice. When we return to Right View, we develop and actualize this faith. We also make use of the other seven practices of the Eightfold Path: Right Intention, Right Action, Right Speech, Right Livelihood, Right Effort, Right Mindfulness, and Right Concentration. Each practice on the Eightfold Path emerges from Right View and then returns the mind to greater confidence and clarity in Right View.

Right View
Home Base for Buddhist Practice

We start with Right View to survey the field of choices, we consider decisions, we make our move, and then we return to home base to evaluate the result of our activity. Returning to Right View involves an important shift to trust our practice with our life. When we take the precepts, we make a vow to live according to Buddhist principles, relying on their teachings rather than relying on our fickle personal perspectives. Right View means we recognize the ego's powerful pull to protect and indulge me and mine, and we "take a backward step" into a spacious room where we may consider the need to acknowledge our own requests or the requests of some very special group to which we believe we belong. We can ask ourselves, "Is this just grasping or is it truly an emergency?" Right View is the mind engaging with a currently perceived threat or attraction, while at the same time maintaining a view of the personal self that is jockeying for supremacy. When we choose to rely on Zen practice and not on the instructions from our personal self, we put practice in charge of our intentions, actions, speech, livelihood or meditation. We consider who or what is observing and what is being observed.

Returning to Right View is a simple step, but with life-changing impact. Taking the backward step is the simple shift from "I'm angry!" to "Anger is arising." When we say, "*I'm* angry!" the one who is angry has merged with and become the anger. When we say, "Anger is arising," we recognize the great space of awareness within which all of our perceptions, sensations, emotions, thoughts, and actions arise. In recognizing or acknowledging the space that is our consciousness, we self-identify with aware space versus the specific emotion presently arising. We say, "I am the space in which anger is arising." This is the activity of Right View, the fruit of practice.

Within our spacious Self, anger has just surfaced. Within that Self or space, we can watch and experience the anger, its connection to some perceived slight or injury, and the demands it might be making for action. The big difference is that the anger does not become a tail wagging the dog; the anger doesn't get its way. What a relief to return to practice in the midst of arising emotions! What a relief not to be controlled by our emotional reactivity! Instead of acting from the arising emotion, we can find Right View and proceed to Right Intention, Right Speech or Right Action. Freedom from habitual patterns is possible.

LIVING RIGHT VIEW
No Rules, No Fixed Positions

The Eightfold Path came to us from early Buddhist practice in India. In early Indian Buddhism, there were many lists of wholesome and unwholesome actions and many rules governing the monks' and nuns' correct conduct. Early Buddhist monks taught the principles of the Eightfold Path and lived in monastic communities observing the many rules (for example not eating after noon) in order to actualize and teach the process of liberation from suffering. But one of Buddhism's unique qualities is the way practice can be changed to become useful wherever it travels. For example, when Buddhism traveled to China, Yunmen Wenyan was able to demonstrate Buddhist practice in terms of Right Action in this moment rather than as correctly following monastic guidelines.

> A monk asked Yunmen: "What is the teaching of the Buddha's entire life time?"
> Yunmen answered: "An appropriate response." (Hartman, 104)

Another translation of Yunmen's answer is "Dancing in tune with the times." Dancing in tune with the times is another way to express the physically active and engaged presence of Right View. The "times" Yunmen speaks of is this very moment. We need to hear this very moment's tune and dance in harmony with it.

As Buddhism moved from India to China, the Zen school became more grounded in actualizing the Eightfold Path and less concerned with summarizing the factors and analyzing the components of the Path. As Zen moved from China to Japan, the ability to manifest compassion and wisdom in and out of the monastery became a hallmark of the Japanese Zen master. Particularly beloved in Japan were Zen teachers who did not look conventionally "holy"; rather, their conduct manifested Yunmen's appropriate response—sometimes even in defiance of formal Buddhist rules.

When we examine esteemed Japanese Zen masters, we find individuals celebrated for the ways they practiced Zen Buddhism to benefit their students and their community rather than as exemplars of perfect monastic practice. In Japan, Zen masters left a rich source of actualized Buddhism—activities off the cushion that embodied the Eightfold Path, but didn't strictly follow monastic guidelines. They were beloved because they were themselves, and like most humans, they had trouble following rules. In his book *Three Zen Masters*, John Stevens writes about Ikkyu Sojun (1394-1481), Hakuin Ekaku (1686-1768), and Ryokan (Taigu Ryokan 1758-1831), three examples of such well-loved and non-conformist Zen masters.

Ikkyu's practice was so well-respected that he was asked to revive the ailing temple complex of Daitokuji in Kyoto. Despite his formal role as abbot, his official portrait pictures him seated beside his mistress. He was unable to observe a Zen abbot's requisite celibacy or to resist eating seafood, and he was honest about his failings while still offering profound Zen leadership and teaching. Quite a lovely Zen dance!

Ryokan was a Zen priest and poet who refused to enter a formal position in either role. Early in his life, he recognized that he could not thrive in monastic life. He preferred life in a solitary hut spiced by playful interactions with village children. His poetry was recorded by the much younger nun, Teishin (1798-1872), with whom he exchanged many love poems. Ryokan also loved to "dance in tune" with local village festivals. He would disguise himself as a woman, wearing a headscarf so he could participate fully in the music and dancing. Everyone recognized Ryokan in disguise, but they also danced along with the masquerade to enjoy his company.

One of the most accomplished Japanese Zen Masters, Hakuin Ekaku, is acknowledged for reviving authentic Rinzai Zen practice in his training monastery, but he is much beloved because of his engagement with the lay people of his village. It is impossible to know what Hakuin was thinking as he met and processed the many complex interactions with his village community; however, given the maturity of his practice, and his response to the following case of a pregnant young woman, it is easy to see his spacious mind and view. His actions during this particular village dispute bring Right View to life.

Hakuin was the priest of a small temple in a rural Japanese village. A beautiful unmarried girl, whose parents owned a food store near him, became pregnant. When her parents discovered her pregnancy, she refused to name the father. After much parental harassment, she insisted that Hakuin, the village priest, was the father.

In great anger the parents went to the master to denounce him for his scandalous behavior as a celibate priest with their daughter. "Is that so?" was all Hakuin would say. When the child was born, the parents brought it to Hakuin, who by now had been discredited by the entire village. They demanded that he take care of the child since it was his responsibility. "Is that so?" Hakuin said calmly and accepted the child. Hakuin provided for himself and the child by begging, taking the child with him on begging rounds.

A year later, the baby's mother could stand it no longer. She told her parents the truth: the real father of the child was a young man who worked in the fish market. The mother and father of the girl went to

31

Hakuin to retrieve the baby, to apologize, and to ask his forgiveness. Hakuin returned the baby that he had undoubtedly come to love over their year together. In handing back the child, all Hakuin said was: "Is that so?"

ACTIVATING RIGHT VIEW
Contemplation

Contemplation is another important aspect of Right View; it is a way we bring Right View to bear on daily life. It is awake, curious, and non-judgmental. We use our attention to review what led to our own stirred-up-ness or the upset of someone else we encountered. Concentration accesses the spacious neutrality of Right View to help us become more present in daily activity.

Perhaps Hakuin was able to maintain his calm responses by combining his practice of Right View with the practice of contemplation. We cannot return to Right View by shutting out our feelings, self-awareness, or personal preferences. Using Zen practice to avoid or repress thoughts and feelings does not result in genuine development in practice nor increased stability of Right View. Practice deepens as we become more intimate with and more accepting of our own dynamic personal experience and reactivity within the "big field." In *Zen Mind, Beginner's Mind*, Suzuki Roshi says: "To give your sheep or cow a large spacious meadow is the way to control him. So it is with people: first let them do what they want, and watch them (19)." This teaching applies not only to cows, sheep, and other people, but also to ourselves—our thoughts and impulses.

Suzuki Roshi taught us to watch our cows, or our own thoughts and impulses, in the big pasture. He instructed us not to ignore these cows nor try to control them. In fact, we may watch these cows, our own thoughts, through the practice of contemplation. When we engage our thoughts by watching them, we enter an interactive relationship with them. It is through this active view that we may change our habits and return to a spacious view.

In contemplation practice, we review or recollect what is happening, who said what, when the trouble started, and what to do next. When first attempting to contemplate a particular event, we might find only a blur or a blank when we search for a neutral position from which to observe. If we use contemplation practice to activate Right View, our awareness will respond to being called upon. As in a sport or physical exercise, when we request an action, the body's response becomes more effective and dependable with repetition. Meditation practice and contemplation practice strengthen each other. As stability of Right View develops in meditation, the observing mind becomes more accessible. Practicing contemplation helps us to strengthen present-moment attention when we return to the cushion for meditation practice.

Using Right View, Hakuin found a way to meet an extremely charged situation without making it worse. He was returning to Right View in his village life. We can practice contemplation in the same way. We can call forth a stop-and-reflect process that occurs somewhere between meditation on the cushion and everyday interactions. The process of contemplation allows us to catch our personal self in the midst of reactivity. Emotional reactivity is one way that this personal and fickle self forcefully and repeatedly insists that we believe in its existence and its central control over our behavior.

In this story about Hakuin, we can imagine him viewing and responding from practice principles rather than reacting instinctively to defend himself from a false accusation. Hakuin's returning to Right View could mean asking himself in the midst of this conversation, "What is this? What is it that I am experiencing? What stirred this up?" and "What now? What does this family want now, and what does my fickle self want now?" Hakuin was working to stay in relationship, "dancing in tune" with this family who had been temple supporters.

Hakuin was wrongly accused, but he saw more than the usual route to self-justification and correction of mistaken beliefs. A conventional personal response might have been to explain to the parents that he was right and they were wrong. Clearly, if he asked himself, "What is this?" he would have realized that there was more at stake than who was telling the truth, more at stake than even Hakuin's virtuous reputation; this young woman's life and her baby's life were at stake. From a spacious position, Hakuin might have asked himself questions that included the young woman's welfare and her family's beliefs. What would happen to this young woman who was going to have a child out of wedlock? Would she be forced from her home? Would she lose her place in society as marriageable? Would she become a prostitute? Would the baby be put up for adoption? By neither refuting nor admitting the parents' claims,

Hakuin gave his cows a "large and spacious meadow." He created time and space—a holding environment for this social and emotional chaos.

If Hakuin had been the baby's father, as a celibate priest and the responsible adult, it would have been appropriate to accept the anger, the blame, and the responsibility for breaking his vows and taking advantage of a young, innocent village girl. Since this was not the case, his job in meeting the conflict was to find Right View, perhaps by pondering, "What does this situation mean to all of us? How will we continue to be in relationship despite this conflict?" Did he recognize that he could probably bear the consequences of this shame more readily than this young woman who brought the shame to his doorstep?

His response—discoverable through contemplation of "What is this?"—enabled a return to Right View, a large and unselfish view of the situation. This view led him to Right Speech. Neither arguing, nor blaming, nor falsely admitting, he simply left the situation open to the next step. By saying, "Is that so?" Hakuin did not argue about the accusation; he awaited the family's ability to consider this matter in their own time. Perhaps the young woman and the father would come forward. Perhaps the family would find a way to make peace with the situation. Hakuin's lack of reactive or defensive response also left space for the family to return to Right View.

Later, when the parents came back with their solution to what they believed to be Hakuin's guilt and responsibility, they insisted that he care for the newborn baby. Perhaps his practice of contemplation in this encounter was "What just happened?" With a baby now in his arms for continued care, he could see that the parents and the daughter were unable to bear the shame of raising an illegitimate infant. Hakuin chose to bear the shame, to be disgraced in the village in their place. He took seriously his priest's role to help his congregation; this demonstrated his Right Intention. Again, he answered, "Is that so?" He did not argue with the parents' assertion that he should raise the child as his responsibility and his punishment. The shame would be ongoing and public. In the practice of contemplation, perceiving "What just happened?" leads to Right View, Right Speech, and then to Right Action. He accepted the infant, and he provided for its care, taking the infant with him on his public begging rounds.

When the parents of the young woman finally learned that Hakuin was not the father of the child, they returned and apologized. How long had Hakuin cared for the infant—for six months or even a year? It's unclear from the story, but surely long enough to learn to love the baby. Through contemplating "What's next?" or "Now what?" Right View and an appropriate response arise. Neither fondness for the child, nor a sense of injustice, nor his legitimate right to scold the parents figured into his response. With a final "Is that so?" the infant was returned to its family.

The ability to contemplate "What's next?" is an important source of human freedom. Being able to freely consider "What's next?" means we are not dragged along by reactivity. Instead we can consider calmly the Right Action for each situation. From a practice perspective, we contemplate what will serve the greater good rather than following our impulse towards defense of the notion of a separate self. Contemplating "What's next?" we can return to Right View. Before we act, we make use of the perspective of Right View that allows us to see our connection with others. We are not shackled to our self-centered view and the continuing suffering it creates. We can begin to enjoy freedom.

Your Life, Your Contemplation, Your Right View

How do we individually activate Right View in our daily lives? Truly, Right View is intensely personal; it is not found through imitation or through robotic following of rules or suppression of feelings. Rather, Right View is activating spacious, flexible mind. Even though we first experience Right View on the meditation cushion, it is through the personal practice of contemplation in daily life that we continue to return to Right View. Right View, like Ryokan, needs to dance in tune within the encounters of personal life. The trick is to learn to balance, to dance gracefully between the principle and the persona. As previously quoted from the Sandokai, *merging with principle*, resting in the view that all is one, *is still not enlightenment*. In fact, an overly emphatic resting in Oneness is a way to avoid reality. Through contemplation, we can actualize Right View by engaging awareness within our daily personal challenges.

Contemplating What?

When we are stressed by a perceived threat or insult, we may feel some agitation, excitement or numbness in the body, followed almost instantaneously by an emotional response. This initial emotional response happens quickly and unconsciously, so the primary threat, and the feeling it provokes, may be obscured. The primary interior feeling could be fear, or anger, or desire, but it is quickly coupled to an automatic secondary exterior emotional response. We move away from the stressor, or against it, or towards it. This emotional machinery is meant to defend us from the perceived threat or insult. It works automatically and at lightning speed.

For example, one's primary emotional response to being attracted to someone might be desire. The interior automatic response might be to want this person to like us, and as a secondary emotional response, we might find ourselves moving toward the person. However, we might also be disposed to an interior experience of hopelessness based on previous loss, and turn away from the attractive person rather than towards them. In the same way, interior hurt feelings can result in an angry exterior reaction or a numbing reaction. By asking "What?" we are trying to discover both the primary feeling and the secondary habitual reaction to it. We tune our awareness to feelings in the body. When we have cultivated Right View and developed a contemplation practice, when we begin to feel some agitation, excitement or numbness in the body, we ask "What?" or "What is this?" Asking "What?" activates the stable concentration and awareness we develop in zazen.

Asking "What?" activates awareness to scan the body-mind equipment. What is my feeling right now? What does it feel like? Does it feel hot or cold, distancing or stirring? Where do I feel this sensation in my body? How long does this feeling last? Does it become more intense and then stop, or does it flash and then gradually disappear? As we bring neutral awareness to feelings in the body, we encourage curiosity and acceptance instead of judgment. If we judge ourselves for what we are feeling, we cover the feeling with additional layers of reactivity. Judgments are a barrier to returning to Right View. Right View is a mindful experience of reality in this moment. The contemplative practice of "What?" stokes our interest in the feeling; we become curious rather than judgmental.

What just happened?

After asking and answering "What?", we can move to contemplation of "What just happened?" In asking "What just happened?" we travel backward in time from this moment to the beginning of the experience, carefully recalling the sequence of events and exchanges. Sometimes this step-by-step rewind helps us to have a more vivid experience of "What?" We may need to review the sequence to catch a more vivid view of what we felt. This activity is different from the activity of meditation; we engage memory to retrace our steps. What sequence of exchanges or actions brought me to this feeling place? While recollection is not part of Zen meditation, during contemplation of "What just happened?" we make use of the clarity developed on the Zen cushion to mentally review the events that led to our current situation and reaction.

When we ask "What just happened?" we are free to respond from Right View—just like Hakuin. If we ask "What just happened?" after an emotional reaction, we can learn what we are afraid of and how we protect ourselves. As we practice this contemplation, we familiarize ourselves with our reactive patterns. We more readily return to Right View rather than remaining stuck in "my" view or "Me, myself and I."

The biologically necessary self would have us believe that it always has our best interests at heart; it seeks to protect us from what just happened or what we fear might happen. Of course, we need a personal self to tell us when it is safe to cross the street, when to eat or sleep and so forth, but it often assumes leadership over our life and our direction. Then, it gathers resources to remain in control. To return to Right View, we contemplate "What just happened?" What is in danger—our pride, our comfort, our possessions, or our life? There are times when it is necessary to protect ourselves, but there are many more moments to contemplate defensiveness and reactivity.

What's next?

The ability to stop and choose "What's next?" is a remarkable event in the process of returning to and stabilizing Right View through contemplation. This question helps us return to and move along the Eightfold Path. When we ask "What's next?" we stand in the present moment with a choice to activate Right Speech and Right Action and to continue on the path of practice. If we don't move towards practice, we may choose instead to activate our selfish habitual response.

All of us begin at an early age to construct a dwelling place to protect ourselves. We choose ways to do this that are consistent with our temperament and circumstances. We construct defensive patterns at about age two. As useful as these resources are for the two-year-old, these reactions, which become habitual, are not that helpful for the wide range of responses necessary for adult life. Established early on, these patterns run automatically in our nervous system. They are activated by a variety of stressors, and they happen swiftly and furiously below conscious level. This means that the defenses we adopted at an early age run our reactions without our conscious cooperation. Being present in the midst of feeling reactivity and being able to ask "What's next?" means we have become conscious of the pattern and its habitual responses. Most importantly, as we look at our old reactivity and consider our other options, we now have choices grounded in the Eightfold Path of practice.

Like fireworks, emotions light up the sky of our mind. Initially, they may flash quickly, yet lead to a longer-lasting reactivity. We might miss the emotion's initial appearance, but if we first practice "What just happened?" and then consider "What's next?", we can more often follow the emotional trace and review the moment the emotion flared. Noting how the sequence unfolded—through remark or action, feeling and re-activity—our own secretly held patterns become known to us. Once we see those patterns and know them, we have the choice to change our response.

RIGHT VIEW
Contemplation in Everyday Practice

The contemplation practice I recommend here is not identical to psycho-therapy. In psychotherapy, we often consider the source of an unhelpful pattern; in contemplation, we assume the source is past experience or temperament, and we focus instead on the pattern of current distress in the present moment. The difference is that in contemplating "What just happened?" we identify the reactivity that caused an emotional or con-flictual response, but we do not need to probe the source of the reaction in childhood memories as we might in psychotherapy. Instead, we can just observe or recall what just happened for a sign of the trigger. Then we can identify the location, quality, and intensity of that feeling in our own body-mind equipment. The questions we ask ourselves are not about why the past experience is connected to our current reaction; instead we ask, "What is it?" or "What just happened?" What did we feel, where did we feel it, what did we say or do when we felt it, and how long did it last? Usually, it is the emotion itself or an unhelpful outcome of our interac-tion that alerts us to consider what just happened.

For some people, contemplation practice may result in increased pain or agitation rather than generating more freedom. When we bring our attention to an old wound or trauma, we may feel overwhelmed by a depth of pain. If increased suffering continues with contemplation practice, psychotherapy may be useful. Some Zen students can be guided skillfully by a therapist through the patterns of suffering they have noted during contemplation. In this way, Zen and psychotherapy may work together to release old patterns and help to generate different options in response to difficult situations and in answering the question "What's next?" with a new dance step. When we practice contemplation, there is a neutral witness who becomes a more reliable observer of the mind and its contents; we can more readily track what just happened. Through contemplation, we learn that emotions can be vivid reminders to return to the path of Right View. Pleasant or unpleasant emotions, like sounds, sensations, or pain in meditation, help us to wake up and notice more in the midst of activity. In contemplating our worldly tasks and relationships, arising emotions are signposts that tell us how to engage, when we have expected too much, and how we are trapped in unwholesome patterns. Emotions are intense and often are felt in the body. They grab our attention more than passing thoughts. Emotions can become physical sensations, such as excitement, pain of loss, rejection, longing, or worry. If we become aware of these sensations, through practicing contemplation, we can explore the arising emotions and their underlying patterns, and we can generate healthier, more appropriate responses.

The practice of zazen is the laboratory in which we keep returning to the spacious field of Right View. We practice the activity while seated and while not actively engaged in daily life. We do this to make the return to Right View our established response. Once returning to Right View has become a regular activity on the cushion, it can be actively engaged in daily life to contemplate "what, what just happened, and what's next." With a neutral, open-minded view of the mind at work during meditation, compassion and curiosity develop naturally. Applying these qualities to our everyday upsets through contemplation practice activates and returns us to the clear-eyed position of Right View. Contemplation paired with Right View allows us to wisely choose our next step and to deepen our commitment on the Eightfold Path.

Works cited

Dogen, Eihei and Kosho Uchiyama. *From the Zen Kitchen to Enlightenment: Refining Your Life*. New York: Weatherhill, 1st ed., 1983.

Hartman, Zenkei Blanche. *Seeds for a Boundless Life: Zen Teachings from the Heart*. Boston: Shambhala, 2015.

Okumura, Shohaku. *Living by Vow*. Boston: Wisdom, 2012.

Stevens, John. *Three Zen Masters*. Tokyo: Kodansha International, 1st ed., 1993.

Suzuki, Shunryu. *Zen Mind, Beginner's Mind*. New York: Weatherhill, 2nd ed., 2000.

Chapter 2

Right Intention: Arousing the Vow of Practice

Zenki Mary Mocine

The second factor on the Noble Path, Right Intention, is *Samyana-samkalpa* in Sanskrit and *Samma-sankappa* in Pali. *Samyana/Samma* is translated usually as "Right" but it can also be translated as wholesome, wise or skillful. *Samkalpa/Sankappa* is usually translated as "Thought" or "Intention" but it can also be translated as resolve, aspiration or the exertion of our own will to change. In this chapter, we will use "Right Intention," because we are not here dealing so much with thinking in the usual sense. Buddhist teacher, Ven. Piyasilo, in *Buddha's Teachings* describes Right Thought as that aspect of the mind that is *conative*, that is, expressing effort or endeavor that requires both thinking and feeling, and he points out that it is:

> [S]ometimes translated as Right Intention, it covers not only the rational ("thinking") aspect but also the emotional ("feeling") aspect. This meaning is best reflected in the Chinese word *xin*, meaning both "heart" and "mind." The unity and balance of both are important in spiritual life. (142-3)

Ven. Sucitto Bhikkhu, in *The Dawn of the Dhamma*, describes Right Intention as the lotus flower, which, like aspiration, grows out of the earth of mundane existence towards the heavens (53). So, Right Intention is very much a practice for our lives. We work through the mess of our heart-minds and in the process we find the lovely lotus flower of liberation.

And what is the Zen approach to Right Intention/Thought? Dogen Zenji wrote in *Shobogenzo* that, "Breaking your meditation pillow is what right thought is about (Hubert 796)." In *Sanjushichihon Bodai Bumpo* (On The Thirty-Seven Methods of Training for Realizing Enlightenment), Dogen Zenji also referred to the notion put forward in his *Fukanzazengi* as: "Think of not-thinking. How do you think of not thinking? Non-thinking. This in itself is the essential art of zazen (Waddell and Abe 4)."

The Zen instruction, then, is to practice hard and practice "non-thinking"—in other words, not getting entangled with thoughts and also not trying to push them away. This is basic zazen, *shikantaza*, simply sitting. Easy to say, difficult to do. Some Zen teachers say simply to sit down, get quiet, and pay attention. I have said this myself.

And yet . . . there is more intentionality to our Zen practice. Many Zen temples do the *Riyaku Fusatsu* or Bodhisattva Ceremony each month, renewing the vows to practice as a bodhisattva and to follow the precepts. We take refuge in Buddha, Dharma, and Sangha and vow not to kill, lie, misuse sexuality, steal, intoxicate self or others, slander, harbor ill will, nor abuse the three treasures. Also, we sit zazen and we can't help but notice unwholesome patterns. We notice how much pain they cause, both to ourselves and to others, when we indulge in unwholesome activities of body, speech, and mind. We resolve to notice deeply, and in the process, we let go of such habits of mind in an organic way because they cause so much difficulty and pain. This is Right Intention in action. However, before we look further to Zen practice regarding this factor on the Path, let us consider what the Buddha himself taught about it.

The Buddha did not flesh out the factors of the Path in his initial teaching. However, he gave us instruction in how to practice with thought in his *Dvedhavitakka Sutta* (Sutra on the Two Sorts of Thinking). Let us turn, then, to this sutra and see that the instruction is familiar to Zen practitioners.

The title refers to the two sorts of thought that the Buddha identified in himself while he was still a bodhisattva. He tells the monks that he divided his thoughts into two sorts: first, unwholesome thoughts of sensuality (desire), ill will, and harmfulness and second, wholesome thoughts of renunciation, loving-kindness, and compassion. He noticed that when thoughts of sense desire arose, they led to affliction for himself or others or both and that such thoughts obstructed his judgment and promoted vexation. They did not lead to liberation. Similarly, with thoughts of ill-will or harmfulness, he realized that they were not useful, were harmful, and did not lead to liberation. When he noticed this, such thoughts tended to subside. When he indulged them, their "habit-force" increased.

The Buddha-to-be noticed that the opposite sorts of thoughts, wholesome thoughts of renunciation, loving-kindness, and compassion did not lead to affliction for himself or others. In fact, they led to liberation. And, by turning toward such thoughts, he found that their "habit-force" increased, leading to peace and joy. And the "habit-force" of the corresponding unwholesome thoughts decreased. Accordingly, the antidote to thoughts of desire or greed is renunciation; to ill-will, the antidote is loving-kindness, and to cruelty, compassion would serve as antidote. (Nanamoli and Bodhi 1-2)

Ven. Sucitto described Right Intention as aspiration. Another word is vow. It seems we need to deeply vow to practice wholesome thought in order to let go of unwholesome thought and manifest the true lotus. Dogen Zenji wrote his words for arousing this vow of practice, the *Eihei Koso Hotsuganmon*:

> We vow with all beings, from this life on throughout countless lives, to hear the True Dharma; that upon hearing it, no doubt will arise in us, nor will we lack in faith; that upon meeting it, we shall renounce worldly affairs and maintain the Buddha Dharma. . . .
>
> Although our past evil karma has greatly accumulated, indeed being the cause and condition of obstacles in practicing the Way, may all Buddhas and Ancestors who have attained the Buddha Way be compassionate to us and free us from karmic effects, allowing us to practice the Way without hindrance. . . .
>
> Quietly explore the farthest reaches of these causes and conditions, as this practice is the exact transmission of a verified Buddha. Confessing and repenting in this way, one never fails to receive profound help from all Buddhas and Ancestors. By revealing and disclosing our lack of faith and practice before the Buddha, we melt away the root of transgressions by the power of our confession and repentance. This is the pure and simple color of true practice, of the true mind of faith, of the true body of faith. (San Francisco Zen Center 2016)

In this moving declaration of his deep intention to practice, Dogen Zenji tells us to own our karmic formations or habits and to explore the causes and conditions that led to our hindrances. We are to "confess and repent," that is, to deeply own them and acknowledge the real harm that arises from our unwholesome habits of mind. We ask for help from our great bodhisattva ancestors and in the process we melt away the very roots of our transgressions.

This aspiration or vow to see our hindrances, own them, and let them go is, I believe, the same as the Buddha's description of his practice in the *Two Kinds of Thought Sutra*. How does this practice operate in each of the kinds of wholesome practice that the Buddha has set out, renunciation, loving-kindness, and compassion? How do we practice with these unwholesome and wholesome sorts of thoughts?

PAYING ATTENTION
Quietly explore the farthest reaches of these causes and conditions . . .

A classic Zen approach begins with paying attention or noticing, particularly noticing the body. When thoughts of desire and greed or ill will or harmful actions arise, what does that feel like in your body? Is there a clenching of the jaw or in the gut? Does your breath get shallow? Is there dis-ease? Is there a grasping after something, a longing? Is there aversion? As the Buddha instructed, it is fundamental to know when such thoughts arise and to know the consequences. Not pleasant. It is natural to want to let go of such thoughts and the associated sensations. It often happens organically, with practice.

Underlying this practice of paying attention are the fundamental practices of generosity and patience. Without generosity, the Way is simply too hard. Generosity is not listed in the Eightfold Path, but it is the first of the *Paramitas* or Perfections of bodhisattva practice in Mahayana Buddhism, of which Zen is a major branch. Patience is the third *Paramita*. It, too, is fundamental to this practice of paying attention. We fail over and over in our intention to let go of unwholesome thoughts and cultivate wholesome ones. We must be patient with ourselves and with others in response to our failings or we will simply give up the effort. Dogen Zenji in "The Bodhisattva's Four Methods of Guidance" explained that generosity is the first of the *Paramitas* because it serves to initiate the process of changing the mind.

> Even when you give a particle of dust, you should rejoice in your own act, because you authentically transmit the merit of all Buddhas, and begin to practice an act of a bodhisattva. The mind of a sentient being is difficult to change. Keep on changing the minds of sentient beings, from the moment that you offer one valuable, to the moment that they attain the way. This should be initiated by giving. Thus, giving is the first of the paramitas.
> (Tanahashi 44)

Dogen reminds us that we are to include ourselves in our giving: "[K]now that to give to yourself is part of giving (45)." In order to change our habits of mind, we must practice generosity with ourselves as well as with others.

The open heart of generosity allows us to give up clinging by a deep vow of renunciation, to give up ill will by actually experiencing loving-kindness for all beings, and to give up the wish to harm by remembering connection in compassion. Patience helps us to stay with this effort even when the practice is daunting.

It is useful then, to address each of the antidotes in more detail. How do we practice renunciation, loving-kindness, and compassion?

RENUNCIATION
We shall renounce worldly affairs and maintain the Buddha Dharma . . .

Renunciation is often described as a letting go. I think of it also as a setting down, as of a burden. When I do full prostration bows, I enact my intention to set down my "ego-burden" and be free of the constant need to protect myself. I renounce it. A full bow is also an enacting of a request for help from the Buddhas and Ancestors or the Universe or however one wants to conceive of a source of support. Zazen itself, of course, is renunciation over and over again. Some periods of zazen feel as if they were an endless session of letting go over and over and over and over, etc. Just a noticing of thinking and a letting it go, sometimes easy and sometimes not so easy.

What are we renouncing? The Buddha referred to noticing thoughts of sense desire or greed. Yes, and. The deepest desire is for existence itself, based on our ignorant self-clinging in our hopeless quest for permanence and independent existence. There is also a parallel desire for non-existence. This is simply another thought of safety and permanence of a different sort. Liberation is letting go of both of these hopeless quests. We will never be "safe" as a permanent event nor safe in nihilism. In those moments when we relax into simple "thisness" we find a deep peace and joy.

When I was sitting with the question of whether or not I truly wanted to be ordained, I went through a difficult discerning process, letting go of many layers of my ego-habits. I saw my desire to please my teacher and to play with the big kids. I saw my desire to be helpful. I saw my ideas about being a priest. Eventually, I let all that go, even the desire to be useful. Oddly, in the end my only concern was not wanting to cut off my hair. I knew I was just using that, but it was a strong feeling of attachment. I told my teacher, Sojun Mel Weitsman Roshi and we spoke of this and that. At the end of our conversation, he said, "One way to make a decision is to act as if you have made it. For instance, why don't you cut off your hair?" I laughed and doubled over as if struck by a blow to my gut and said something rude. We laughed and I left. I went up to the zendo at Tassajara and sat by myself. I cried and then felt a floating sensation and it was over. I had let the last hesitation go and cutting my hair became a joy. This is the joy of renunciation. When it is thorough, it is often joyous.

The joy of renunciation is not necessarily happy; it is deeper than happiness. There is a lightness to it as the burden of desire has been set down. This work of melting the root of our transgressions is not always easy. It can be hard work, but it is necessary and useful work.

Desire and longing can possess us. One can become obsessed, for example, with lust for a happily married friend. Our meditation becomes torture as thoughts and fantasies of desire arise, are set aside, and immediately arise again. It is easy for someone else to say, "Just let it go. Those are just thoughts, empty of substance. There is no self. No other. Think of renunciation." It is easy to tell yourself, "I should let this go. This is not useful. This is harmful. I would never act on these feelings." Not so easy to let such thoughts and feelings go. In fact, hysterical laughter might be the appropriate response to glib advice, even from yourself.

How do we find our way to renunciation when the desire is strong? We practice exploration, just as Dogen Zenji advises in the *Eihei Koso Hotsuganmon*. Explore the causes and conditions of your hindrance. In zazen, we let go of thinking, maybe ten thousand times in a period, or so it seems. We notice when the lustful thoughts arise. Sometimes we indulge in fantasies. We notice that. We do not judge. If we judge, we notice that. Useful, eh? Beating up on yourself is just another layer of desire. Aversion is just another aspect of desire. "I" am a bad, selfish, lustful, greedy person and so on. Instead, over and over we practice letting go of the story. Come back to the body. What is the sensation under the lust? Explore. Is there tightness? Tears? Heat? An impulse to cringe? Explore. Where is your breath? This exploration can become more interesting than the lust if done wholeheartedly. Explore the fact that things do change.

One day, as if by magic, the desire will lift and you may even wonder whatever led you to such feelings. Perhaps your friendship will deepen but without the burden of lust. Even if there is a slight regret, there will be the kind of lightness and joy that I have described. *This is the pure and simple color of true practice, of the true mind of faith, of the true body of faith.*

Be an explorer in the realm of renunciation. It does take courage to deeply look at what is going on, but it does get easier. Sometimes folks who are new to meditation notice their hindrances and feel that they have become a terrible person. The truth is that they have just stopped distracting themselves and have begun the process of really seeing. They are becoming explorers. We can strengthen our ability to explore by exercising our "discernment muscle." Then we can use it to see clearly and, in the process, find the courage to let go of unwholesome habits of mind. We can come to see our true wholesome nature as bodhisattvas.

There is an ancient story from the *Lotus Sutra* that is encouraging for explorers in the discernment realm. The chapter is often named "Faith Discernment." It is a prodigal son story. A young man born to a noble family goes astray; pulled by sense desire, he becomes a drunk and wastrel. He wanders about and loses all sense of himself. His father searches for him, with no success. One day, it happens that the father is outside his palace, receiving gifts from his subjects. The son has wandered home but does not even know where he is. He is simply begging, hoping maybe to get something from all the gifts and celebration. The father instantly sees and knows his son and sends retainers to bring him home. When they touch the young man, he gets very upset, crying out that he is innocent and has done nothing. He faints. The father tells the retainers to let the boy go and to follow him into the village and find where he is staying. They do, and the next day the father sends his steward to offer the boy work shoveling manure in the stables and to tell him he will be paid, housed, clothed, and fed. The boy accepts and is treated well and begins to work well. After a bit, he is given cleaner work, and he continues to do well. From time to time his father works with him and encourages him. The young man steadily improves and works hard and eventually is given work inside the palace and more responsibility. Finally, he is made the majordomo of the whole grand estate and the palace and has charge of all that his father possesses. One day, his father takes him into the treasure room and tells him, "This is all yours. You are my son." The young man has grown to the point that he can finally accept this news. (Kato, Tamura and Miyasaka 110-125)

Of course, this story is about accepting his Buddha Nature, not about material goods. The point is that when we dig through our own manure and exercise our own faith discernment muscle and learn to explore, we develop our own ability to see. We develop our faith in our own ability to practice. It gets easier.

It is just this exploration that supports our intention to give up self-clinging. As we see our unwholesome thoughts and their unfortunate consequences, we develop the deep vow to let them go, to renounce them. And, at the same time, we begin to see our bodhisattva nature and to be able to rejoice in it. Again, this generous view supports our intention to renounce unwholesome habits of mind. To paraphrase Dogen Zenji, give your true self to your true self.

LOVING-KINDNESS
Discover the element of good in your enemy.

Loving-kindness (*metta*) is the antidote when our thinking is characterized by ill will. Loving-kindness is the benevolent wishing well for all beings. In the *Maharahulovada Sutta* (Greater Exhortation to Rahula Sutra), the Buddha told his son, Rahula, that when ill will arose, he should practice the contemplation of loving-kindness: "[F]or when you develop the meditation on loving-kindness, any ill will will be abandoned (Nanamoli and Bodhi 530)."

So we should keep practicing loving-kindness as often as possible, given how often ill will arises. The Buddha's words on loving-kindness are particularly represented in the *Metta Sutta* (Sutra on Loving-Kindness). The Buddha taught it to a group of monks who were distracted by ill will directed at them. It includes a prayer in the middle:

> May all beings be happy. May we be joyous and live in safety. All living beings, whether weak or strong, in high or middle or low realms of existence, small or great, visible or invisible, near or far, born or to be born, may all beings be happy. Let no one deceive another, nor despise any being in any state; let none by anger or hatred wish harm to another (San Francisco Zen Center 2016).

Note that the quote asks that "we" be joyous. It does not say "they," because our wish for the well-being of all must include ourselves. I changed the translation that we use at Clear Water Zendo from "they" to "we" to emphasize this point. You must include yourself. My experience is that people are harshest and most vitriolic to themselves. Years ago I led a class at Tassajara Zen Mountain Monastery, and we did an exercise. I asked the people to look around and note everyone in the room, then close their eyes and think of something nice about each person. When they opened their eyes, I asked if anyone had included themselves. Not one had done so, and there were thirty people in the room.

The classic text on loving-kindness is found in the *Visuddhimagga* (The Path of Purification), an ancient text by Bhadantacariya Buddhagosa. It is a compendium of the Buddha's teaching, written in 412 CE. The most well-known section is the "Four *Brahmaviharas*" or Divine Abodes: loving-kindness, compassion, gladness and equanimity (Nanamoli 321-343). The introduction to the section on loving-kindness advises that the meditator: "[S]hould embark upon the development of lovingkindness for the purpose of secluding the mind from hate seen as a danger and introducing it to patience known as an advantage (321)."

The initial practice suggested is meditation on loving-kindness, beginning with oneself. Classic *metta* meditations begin with wishing oneself well, happy, at ease, perhaps after first opening the heart by thinking of someone loved and in difficulty, but the exercise begins with taking oneself into the heart. This can be done at any time that seems good to you, maybe at the beginning or end of the day, or just before zazen. The following is a simple version that you may try. There are many in books and examples online as well. Begin by closing your eyes and settling your mind. After each line of the meditation, stop to notice how that action or statement feels in your body.

> Take yourself into your heart.
> Say to yourself, "May I be well, happy and safe."
> Take someone you are close to into your heart.
> Say to that person, "May you be well, happy and safe."
> Take someone about whom you feel neutral into your heart.
> Say to that person, "May you be well, happy and safe."
> Take someone who is difficult for you into your heart.
> Say to that person, "May you be well, happy and safe."
> Take this group or your community into your heart.

Say to the group, "May we be well, happy and safe."
Take yourself into your heart.
Say to yourself, "May I be well, happy and safe."

Often there is not much sensation when you first start doing such a meditation but if you do it regularly, over time it opens up. It is very useful and interesting to notice the sensations around someone who is difficult for you, towards whom you feel ill will. I remember feeling the person squirming and angry to be held by me. This changed over time, and my feelings regarding that person changed and lightened as well. This is exactly the practice of noticing and owning that the Buddha and Dogen Zenji describe.

A simple version of *metta* is to begin one's first period of zazen in a day by saying a short *metta* prayer to oneself. I do this every morning as I begin: "May all beings, all of us, all around without limit, particularly, (list of maybe 4-8 names, including someone difficult for me, when that is up, and ending with myself), be well, happy, at ease." It sets my intention for the day and opens my heart.

In the Divine Abode Loving-Kindness text, the longest section, "Getting Rid of Resentment," has to do with how to practice with those one finds difficult, towards whom one feels resentment (Nanamoli 324-332). It seems even two thousand years ago, as now, this was a very common theme in human lives. Many practices are offered to the practitioner wanting to establish herself in loving-kindness. One looks at how hating harms the hater and makes the hater ugly in others' eyes. One considers something about the other that is admirable. If there is nothing, then perhaps compassion may be aroused. Or one should remember that one is creating unwholesome karma through anger. One could give a gift and find that resentment abates. One can recall the Buddha's forbearance in past lives. And, one can recall the eleven blessings to be expected from the cultivation of loving-kindness:

> A man sleeps in comfort, wakes up in comfort, and dreams no evil dreams, he is dear to human beings, he is dear to non-human beings, deities guard him, fire and poison and weapons do not affect him, his mind is easily concentrated, the expression of his face is serene, he dies unconfused, if he penetrates no higher he will be reborn in the Brahma World. (Nanamoli 331)

In 1957, a modern Master, Martin Luther King, Jr., addressed these same issues in a sermon at Dexter Avenue Baptist Church in Montgomery, Alabama. He had taken as his text Jesus' admonition to "Love your enemies." Dr. King pointed out that this is difficult but also very practical advice. Like Buddhagosa and the Buddha before him, he pointed out how hating harms the hater. He also spoke of an important first step, paraphrasing Jesus, to look at yourself and think if you have done something to contribute to any resentment directed at you. Jesus said not to worry about the splinter in another's eye but to worry instead about the board in your own. I have an article of faith, confirmed over and over in practice, that it is never just one person's fault when difficulty arises. I always have some responsibility when conflict arises. Dr. King did not speak of karma, but like the Buddha and Buddhagosa, he asked us to consider the true nature of all beings (divine nature/Buddha nature) and the deep importance of non-harming.

> And when you come to the point that you look in the face of every man and see deep down within him what religion calls the "image of God," you begin to love him in spite of *[sic]*. No matter what he does, you see God's image there. And there is an element of goodness that he can never slough off. Discover the element of good in your enemy. And as you seek to hate him, find the center of goodness and place your attention there and you will take a new attitude.
>
> Another way that you love your enemy is this: when the opportunity presents itself for you to defeat your enemy, that is the time which you must not do it. There will come a time, in many instances, when the person who hates you most, the person who has misused you most, . . . there will come a time when you will have an opportunity to defeat that person. It might be in terms of a recommendation for a job. It might be in terms of helping that person to make some move in life. That's the time you must do it! That is the meaning of love. In the final analysis, love is not this sentimental something that we talk about. It is not merely an emotional something. Love is creative, understanding goodwill for all men. It is the refusal to defeat any individual. When you rise to the level of love, of its great beauty and power, you seek only to defeat evil systems. (King, para 14-15)

These are powerful words. They are challenging words. King admonishes us to follow them as practical advice. The world will not change unless we form the intention to deeply see and deeply know the true nature of our fellow human beings. We simply must let go of ill will and we simply must practice loving-kindness. The more we know the harm from the habit-force of the former, the stronger our intention to develop habit-force of the latter.

The practices of thinking about and knowing the harm from ill will, knowing our own responsibility for enmity with another, seeing the Buddha Nature of all beings, non-harming, recitation of the *Metta Sutta*, and engaging in *metta* meditations are the foundations of loving-kindness.

Again, we practice in our zazen by simply noticing. If thoughts of anger and resentment arise, if we tend to harbor ill will, we must be aware of them. No need to think about them nor get on their train of thought. Just notice. Just check the body and its sensations. No story, just exploring what is happening. Is your jaw tight? How about your shoulders? Is your face flushed? Explore. Heart racing? Mind going a mile-a-minute? Explore. Where is your breath? Again, no self-blaming, just noticing. If you must criticize yourself, notice that, and see if you can at least refrain from criticizing yourself for criticizing yourself. Oh well. Just notice. It all feels lousy, doesn't it? Keep noticing and maybe you will get tired of hurting yourself in this way. Maybe you will be able to refrain from expressing your ill will to others. Maybe you will believe your story less. Maybe you will be able to make amends more easily if you have demonstrated your ill will. Keep exploring and owning.

In Mahayana practice, we return to the marketplace. We do not stay on the cushion forever. We take the zazen mind out into the world. So, we use the habits of mind around loving-kindness that we have developed on the cushion, and we go to work, or home, or out with friends. We use our strengthened ability to notice unwholesome habits and thoughts of ill will, and we are more able to let them go, to refrain from expressing them. We can more easily remember the love available for all people and remember we do not want to harm the one we're with. As we practice out in the world and see the strength of our habits of mind, we deepen our intention to develop the wholesome habit-force of loving-kindness.

COMPASSION
May all Buddhas and ancestors . . . be compassionate to us . . .

The practice of compassion is the Buddha's antidote to thoughts of cruelty and harm. Sometimes our thoughts of ill will are so strong that we actually want to harm another. We want to inflict suffering or, at the least, we don't care if we inflict suffering. Compassion means "to suffer with," and it is the wish to save all beings from suffering. It is the second Divine Abode.

Buddhagosa advises us to arouse the thought of compassion by imagining someone who is suffering and to use that image to open our hearts and feel for the suffering one (Nanamoli 340). The practice regarding difficulty with opening one's heart is basically the same as for loving-kindness: notice how unwholesome thoughts, here of cruelty or harming, feel in the body. Notice how very harmful they can be, and how they harm oneself as well as others. Notice the strength of the habit-force and its destructive power. Notice that such habitual thoughts of harm tend to arise out of one's own difficulties and karmic causes and conditions. Use this noticing to strengthen one's intention to engage in wholesome thought-habits of compassion for the suffering of others. As with loving-kindness, again, include oneself. Our compassionate response to suffering must begin with ourselves.

Years ago, when I was at Tassajara, Tenshin Reb Anderson Roshi gave a lecture about compassion. He defined it as "Stay close and do nothing." Yes. When we stay close, we know the connection with self and other. We know what is going on inside ourselves, be it anger, a wish to harm, a wish to flee, fear, guilt, or perhaps sadness. Once we know, we can respond to our unwholesome mind-habit and take care of ourselves with compassion. When we stay close, we can know what is going on with another. We can listen and respond.

When we respond, it can come from "doing nothing." It can arise organically from the heart of compassion rather than from some idea or view of what "should" be done. Sometimes we say to "respond" rather than "react." Reacting here is defined as the activity of acting from view or one's own attachment or need to self-protect. Responding arises organically and happens without self-regard. It is non-doing.

At one point I told Tenshin Roshi about an experience that I had had at an Al-Anon meeting. I sat beside a woman who was sharing something very difficult. She was crying as she spoke. I kept thinking that I "should" do something, take her hand, touch her shoulder or something, but I held back. At the end of such a meeting, everyone stands and holds hands to say the closing dedication. As we ended, she and I turned to one another, and I took her in my arms and she sobbed. It was not thought out. It seemed to just happen. Tenshin Roshi said to remember the experience as emblematic. It has served me as a reminder of what it is to simply respond. When the time was right, my heart opened and the appropriate response arose. No doing.

This example from the Al-Anon meeting is useful to demonstrate non-doing and responding, but what about when we are troubled by unwholesome thoughts of harming or even cruelty? They can exert a strong habit-force over our thought process. We can begin by staying very close to them. It is not necessary to act but it is necessary to know that they are present. Stay close. Turn towards such unwholesome thoughts. Usually there are layers of feeling below the angry ones. When we turn towards the body and get quiet and ask, "What is this?" we often see that the anger arises from hurt and/or fear. The practice of getting to know these feelings can be much more interesting than the thoughts of anger or revenge. This is exactly the practice or expression of Right Intention.

As you get to know your suffering, compassion for yourself naturally arises. It may take some patient practice to sit still for your suffering and for what underlies it, but eventually there may be a softening. As you soften to your own suffering, you can begin to see that all beings suffer as well. You are not different. Your compassionate heart can open to all beings. Just as you do not want to suffer, you can see in your heart that nobody wants to suffer. This will strengthen your vow to encourage wholesome thoughts and to let go of unwholesome ones, in this case, harming.

As you see that you are not different from all beings, you can see that you are deeply connected. Compassion arises organically from this realization. You don't want to hit your own thumb with a hammer, after all. So, if we are one, you and I, we don't want to hurt ourself.

We can encourage ourselves in this practice of compassion with the image of the eleven-headed Avalokiteshvara, the bodhisattva of compassion—the hearer of the cries of the world. One version of why she has so many heads is that she kept having to grow another when her prior head exploded. This happened when she went down to the hell-realm and saved all the suffering beings there. She helped the last one out and waved goodbye. Avalokiteshvara turned back to enjoy the sight of the empty hell and . . . it was full! Her head exploded. This happened ten times before she understood that saving all beings is just what she does. Or, she "no-does." She simply responds to the suffering. We can use this story to support our own practice to see the suffering and to simply respond.

Developing Right Intention can seem daunting. If we cannot simply "legislate" it, or think about it, it may seem overwhelming. The practices discussed here are meant to be encouraging. We can develop Right Intention only by enacting it over and over, by putting our intention on paying attention to our unwholesome habits of mind and thus finding the motivation to let them go. As we see the harm from unwholesome habits of mind, wholesome habits will organically arise, and we can find the will to nurture loving-kindness and compassion.

The following words from the beginning of Archarya Buddharak-khita's translation of *The Dhammapada* (The Collected Sayings of the Buddha) are a great support in our effort to deepen our intention to practice renunciation, loving-kindness, and compassion in our heart-minds:

1. Mind precedes all mental states. Mind is their chief; they are all mind-wrought. If with an impure mind a person speaks or acts, suffering follows him like the wheel that follows the foot of the ox.

2. Mind precedes all mental states. Mind is their chief; they are all mind-wrought. If with a pure mind a person speaks or acts, happiness follows her like her never-departing shadow.

3. "He abused me, he struck me, he overpowered me, he robbed me." Those who harbor such thoughts do not still their hatred.

4. "He abused me, he struck me, he overpowered me, he robbed me." Those who do not harbor such thoughts still their hatred.

5. Hatred is never stilled by hatred in this world. By non-hatred alone is hatred appeased. This is a law eternal. (23)

Works cited

Buddhagosa, Bandantacariya. *The Path of Purification:Visuddhimagga.* Trans. Bhikkhu Nanamoli. Vipassana Meditation and the Buddha's Teachings. Onalaska, WA: Parayati Publishing, 2003.

Buddharakkhita, Archarya, trans. *The Dhammapada: The Buddha's Path of Wisdom.* Tullera, Australia: Buddha Dharma Education Assoc., 1985.

Dogen, Eihei. "The Bodhisattva's Four Methods of Guidance." *Moon in a Dewdrop: Writings of Zen Master Dogen.* Kazuaki Tanahashi, ed. and trans. Berkeley, CA: North Point, 1985.

---. "Eihei Koso Hotsuganmon (Great Ancestor Dogen's Verse for Arousing the Vow)." *San Francisco Zen Center.* San Francisco Zen Center, 2016. Web. 26 Apr. 2016. <https://sanfranciscozencenter.blob.core.windows.net/assets/29_Eihei_Koso_Hotsuganmon.pdf>

---. "On the Thirty-Seven Methods of Training for Realizing Enlightenment." *Shobogenzo: The Treasure House of the Eye of the True Teaching.* Hubert Nearman, trans. Mt. Shasta, CA: Shasta Abbey Press, 2007.

Kato, Bunno, Yoshiro Tamura and Kojiro Miyasaka, trans. "Faith Discernment." *The Threefold Lotus Sutra.* Tokyo: Kosei Publishing Co., 1975.

King, Martin Luther, Jr. "Loving Your Enemies." Dexter Avenue Baptist Church, Montgomery, AL. 17 Nov. 1957. Stanford University. "Martin Luther King, Jr. and the Global Freedom Struggle." *The Martin Luther King, Jr. Research and Education Institute, King Encyclopedia.* Stanford University, n.d. Web. 26 Apr. 2016. <kingencyclopedia.stanford.edu/encyclopedia/documentsentry/doc_loving_your_enemies.1.html>

Metta Sutta (Loving Kindness Meditation). *San Francisco Zen Center.* San Francisco Zen Center, 2016. Web. May 2016. <https://sanfranciscozencenter.blob.core.windows.net/assets/11_Loving_Kindness_Meditation.pdf>

Nanamoli, Bhikkhu and Bhikkhu Bodhi, trans. "Dvedhavitakka Sutta (Sutra on Two Sorts of Thinking)." MN 19. and "Maharahulovada Sutta (Greater Exhortation to Rahula Sutra)." MN 62. *The Middle Length Discourses of the Buddha: A translation of the Majjhima Nikaya* (Teachings of the Buddha). Somerville, MA: Wisdom, 1995.

Piyasilo, Thera. *Buddha's Teachings: A Study of Comparative Buddhism in Truth, Tradition and Transformation.* Petaling Jaya, Malaysia: Dharmafarer Enterprises, 1991.

Sucitto, Bhikkhu. *The Dawn of the Dhamma: Illuminations from the Buddha's First Discourse*. Bangkok: Buddhadhamma Foundation, 1996.

Waddell, Norman and Masao Abe. *The Heart of Dogen's Shobogenzo*. Albany, NY: State Univ. of NY Press, 2002.

CHAPTER 3

Right Speech: The Dance of Understanding
Tonen O'Connor

"And what bhikkhus, is right speech? Abstinence from false speech,
abstinence from divisive speech, abstinence from harsh speech,
abstinence from idle chatter: this is called right speech."
—The Buddha, as quoted in an early text, the *Samyutta Nikaya* (Bodhi 1528)

The components of the Eightfold Path are generally divided into three sections: Wisdom (*Prajna*), Concentration (*Samadhi*) and Ethics (*Sila*), with Right Speech falling under *Sila*. For this reason, it may be useful to think about what we mean by the word "ethics." My dictionary defines ethics as moral principles that govern the behavior of a person or group and gives Judeo-Christian ethics as an example. This is very interesting because it suggests that there is no universal ethical or moral code, but that an ethic has its roots in the deepest beliefs of a particular group, often linked to their religion, which raises the question of why speech is specifically included in Buddhist ethics. I think it may be because speech is an action driven by our understanding of the nature of the world in which we exist and by our desire to communicate that understanding. Buddhists have a particular and very deep understanding of our world as completely interdependent and constantly changing. Our ethical behavior is grounded in this understanding, rather than in a belief in an unchanging and permanently given set of principles. We live within complex, constantly altering relationships. I'm changing, you're changing, everything is changing.

As I look at this, I see that however we approach speech, we must be light of foot, engaging in the dance of changing understandings. We need to be aware not only of what we say, but how we react to what others say. Our intentions may be good, their intentions may be good, and we may still find hurt in the air.

I'm reminded of an innocent enough exchange that occurred many years ago in the corridors of the Performing Arts Center (PAC) where the Milwaukee Repertory Theater, of which I was the managing director, was housed at that time. I was walking with the business manager, also a woman, when we encountered a staff member from the PAC. "Good afternoon, ladies," he cheerfully remarked. "Good afternoon," said we, and then the business manager turned to me and said angrily, "I'm not a LADY!" The staff member meant to be cheerful and kind, yet he used a word the business manager found offensive. Her resentment blinded her to his good intentions and his good intentions did not help him see that the word "lady" carried some baggage when applied to a woman proud of her business acumen. It's a delicate business.

It is, of course, possible to see the Eightfold Path as primarily an antidote to our personal suffering, as the means to realize the promise of liberation given in the Third Noble Truth if we live in accordance with the components of the path. It is, however, more than that. Buddhist ethics are deeply rooted in the Buddha's teaching on impermanence and interdependence. If we are to fully embody the Eightfold Path in a "right" manner, our life must be lived in light of the deep truth of reality as constant change and as a web of relationships. This is the nature of our true self, ever-changing and inextricably engaged in the life of the whole. To manifest this understanding, we utilize Right Speech, embracing a beneficial approach to our myriad relationships with others.

This means that we must be cautious in how we understand "right," for it must not represent a clutch of too particular and absolute admonitions. Nothing is always right or always wrong. Even if it is so ninety-nine out of a hundred times, we must be prepared to realize the hundreth instance. I tend to prefer the modifier "correct" to "right" and sometimes find myself going on to say that I mean "appropriate," that is, fitting and beneficial to the circumstance at hand. Context should define correct speech, and appropriate speech is made up of several elements, most of which must be present before we can say that it is beneficial.

The Buddha was very aware of this complexity, as you will see from the selection below. It seems repetitive; yet as we read it, we begin to realize the subtlety of the Buddha's reasoning. For speech to be *samma vaca* or perfect, clear, and wholesome, one must pay close attention.

In the *Abhayarajakumara Sutta*, the Buddha says:

So, too, prince, such speech as the Tathagata knows to be untrue, incorrect and unbeneficial, and which is also unwelcome and disagreeable to others: such speech the Tathagata does not utter. Such speech as the Tathagata knows to be true and correct but unbeneficial, and which is also unwelcome and disagreeable to others: such speech the Tathagata does not utter. Such speech as the Tathagata knows to be true, correct, and beneficial, but which is unwelcome and disagreeable to others, the Tathagata knows the time to use such speech. Such speech as the Tathagata knows to be untrue, incorrect and unbeneficial, but which is welcome and agreeable to others, such speech the Tathagata does not utter. Such speech as the Tathagata knows to be true and correct but unbeneficial, and which is welcome and agreeable to others, such speech the Tathagata does not utter. Such speech as the Tathagata knows to be true, correct and beneficial, and which is welcome and agreeable to others: the Tathagata knows the time to use such speech. Why is that? Because the Tathagata has compassion for beings. (Nanamoli and Bodhi 500)

"Compassion for beings"—such a simple way of pointing to the impulse that lies behind Right Speech. It is this compassion that lies at the heart of the Eightfold Path, an empathy that understands that we have no separate self, and that we draw our being from our intimate relationship with the people who surround us and from the environment in which we live. Even if something has the ingredients and meets the conditions necessary to Right Speech, the Buddha suggests that, out of compassion for living beings, it is not fully Right Speech unless it is delivered at the appropriate moment for, among other things, it may not be really heard or absorbed if the time is not ripe.

Am I concerned here only with what I say? Is this section of the Eightfold Path solely about the words issuing from my mouth? Considered in the fullness of its reach, speech embraces a wide assortment of direct communication. In the most popular romance novels, the heroine's eyes always speak volumes and the hero's gestures whisper of love. To really think about "speech" we must include nonverbal modes of communication such as gesture, behavior, and demeanor. Even when we think we are not saying anything, we are communicating who we are.

I'm always startled when I'm in France and someone approaches me and immediately speaks English. I'm not in a tourist group. I'm navigating the metro with ease, reading directions in French. I resemble a bit my Alsatian great-grandfather, and yet, and yet, the way I stand, the way I move through space, everything about me shouts, "American!" I once rode the metro in Paris in a car holding many North Africans, and immediately picked out a woman as American. Stepping down onto the platform, she said to me, "Are you an American?" "Yes," I replied, "and I think you are, too." She was African-American and dark-skinned, yet her bearing said very clearly "American," as did mine. By merely looking at one another, we had a conversation of sorts. This is also why it's difficult to deliver loving words from an angry face. A kind of deceit becomes obvious when our words and demeanor do not match. As we continue our examination of Right Speech, let's think broadly enough to go beyond communication with words, although words have special pride of place, and we must examine closely their impact.

Words themselves live in written as well as spoken form, so as we search for appropriate communication, we must look hard at the written word, these days ubiquitously encountered via both the printed word and electronic media. As I write these words, I am speaking with you, the reader, just as surely as if we faced one another over a cup of coffee. There is one difference, of course. You cannot see my face or hear the intonation and inflection of my voice. This is why humor and sarcasm so often fall flat over the Internet, no matter how many cute little emoticons we utilize. This is also why the Internet is the source of so much misunderstanding. We can open our mouths by whipping off missives on our computers with an ease that does not encourage thought or the weighing of words as in the old days of handwritten letters.

Encouragement of Right Speech is found in a number of Buddhist texts. To return to the Buddha's statements in the *Abhayarajakumara Sutta*, Right Speech is "true, correct and beneficial, . . . welcome and agreeable to others." From this foundation, direct instructions concerning our behavior were formulated. The Fourth Precept, accepted as guidance by those who are entering the Buddha's sangha, says in the translation I use: "A disciple of the Buddha abstains from speaking falsely." Above all, Right Speech must be factual in nature and true to the emotional states of both speaker and hearer—no embroidering for effect, no glossing over unpleasantness, no outright fabrication—and we must be aware of whether or not this is the moment to say these particular words. My life is inextricably bound with yours and, recognizing this, I must not blurt out hastily something inappropriate to the moment. A millisecond spent in assessing the nature of those receiving our words and the probable impact of those words on them may prevent hours of regret.

One would think it fairly easy to assess the factual nature of something we are about to say, but in actuality it can be a very dicey matter indeed. Exactly what is the source of my idea that this is a fact? How reliable is that source? Surely not because everyone says it's so. Remember the Buddha's admonition to the Kalamas in the *Kalama Sutta*:

> Come, Kalamans, do not be satisfied with hearsay or with tradition or with legendary lore or what has come down in your scriptures or with conjecture or with logical inference or with weighing evidence or with liking for a view after pondering over it or with someone else's ability or with the thought, "The monk is our teacher." When you know in yourselves: "These ideas are unwholesome, liable to censure, condemned by the wise, being adopted and put into effect they lead to harm and suffering," then you should abandon them. . . . Come, Kalamans, do not be satisfied with hearsay or with the thought "The monk is our teacher." When you know in yourselves "These things are wholesome . . . " then you should practice and abide in them. (Nanamoli 175-76)

Nor is social media a reliable resource. Just because someone says something on Facebook is no guarantee of truth. My daily newspaper has a feature called Politifact, which is derived from a national research effort that uses multiple resources to smoke out the factual or non-factual nature of a statement. It occasionally tackles some allegation that has gone viral on the Internet and hence been accepted by thousands as fact. Often there is zero basis in fact; the entire statement is fiction. I'm reminded of the power of words to validate themselves. Nazi propaganda minister Joseph Goebbels is reputed to have said that if you say something forcefully enough, often enough, and keep doing so, it will become viewed as fact.

Then there is the problem of whether to say something that is factual, yet contrary to the belief of the person addressed and perhaps thereby unbeneficial. During a meeting with one of the Milwaukee Zen Center's prison sanghas, we discussed how we might be able to abide by the precept against speaking falsely when we know that the truth will hurt. I posed a hypothetical situation, which one of the inmates later said that he had actually experienced. Here's the dilemma:

> You have a dear friend who is in the hospital in the final stages of a terminal illness. You receive a call from the hospital saying

that he will die within a few hours, and urging you to see him as soon as possible. You rush to the hospital and, with deep concern for the impending loss, you enter his room. You expect to find him at the end, yet with a burst of unexpected energy, he looks up at you and says, "You know, I think I'm going to make it!" What do you say?

The truth is that he will NOT make it, yet to say this is cruel. To say something like, "You bet you are! You'll be out of here in no time!" is false. We agreed that what could be said is, "I'm glad you feel that way," speaking to the truth of your response, not the objective fact.

Further, if we are to fully consider Right Speech, we must also consider Right Silence. It is this Right Silence that comes into being when the Tathagata refrains from saying something untrue or something true but hurtful. I always brace myself when someone says, "The truth is . . . ," for it inevitably means they have something unpleasant to say such as: "The truth is, you can no longer wear that dress size."

I think that Right Silence also means not participating in what the Buddha calls malicious speech or idle chatter. If we hope to be on the Path, we need to hold back from gossip about others, rumor, or needless speculation. In the realm of speculation, sometimes we seem convinced that if we discuss in great detail what may happen, we are speaking the truth. We love to predict, when it might be better to just keep our mouths shut in Right Silence. Spreading rumors takes advantage of the gullibility and lack of knowledge on the part of others, and depends on what a member of our prison sangha once described as "inmate.com."

Speech is one of the most effective means we have for influencing others. A bodhisattva aspires to be a buddha without retreating to the bliss of nirvana, but rather remaining active in the world to free all beings from suffering. The first of the Four Great Bodhisattva Vows is: "Beings are numberless, I vow to free them." Given this vow, the means at the disposal of the bodhisattva are of utmost importance. Among them is *priya-akhyana* or kind speech. This is where the Buddha's sympathy for living beings, as expressed in the *Abhayarajakumara Sutta* comes into play.

Dogen Zenji, in the *Shobogenzo* fascicle *Bodaisatta-shishobo* (Four Elements of a Bodhisattva's Social Relations), discusses four means a bodhisattva utilizes to create and maintain beneficial relationships that will lead others onto the Path. Here Dogen defines kind speech:

"Kind speech," means, when meeting living beings, first of all to feel compassion for them and to offer caring and loving words. Broadly, it is there being no rude or bad words. In secular societies there are polite customs of asking others if they are well. In Buddhism there are the words, "Take good care of yourself!" and there is the disciple's greeting, "How are you?" Speaking with the feeling of compassion for living beings as if they were babies is kind speech. We should praise those who have virtue and should pity those who lack virtue. Through love of kind speech, kind speech is gradually nurtured. Thus, kind speech which is ordinarily neither recognized nor experienced manifests itself before us. While the present body and life exist we should enjoy kind speech, and we will not regress or deviate through many ages and many lives. Whether in defeating adversaries or in promoting harmony among gentlefolk, kind speech is fundamental. To hear kind speech spoken to us directly makes the face happy and the mind joyful. To hear kind speech indirectly etches an impression in the heart and in the soul. Remember, kind speech arises from a loving mind, and the seed of a loving mind is compassion. We should learn that kind speech has the power to turn around the heavens; it is not merely the praise of ability. (Nishijima and Cross 3:31)

Dogen speaks of our pleasure in hearing kind speech. There is also great pleasure in utilizing kind speech. This is true even with the stock phrases we use, such as "Have a nice day!" This reminds me of my conversation with a British theater director who came to direct a play at the Milwaukee Repertory Theater. He was quite taken with our various Americanisms, but one day said to me in disgust, "You're always saying 'Have a nice day!' and it doesn't mean anything!" "Yes," I responded, "and when I've been in England, I've found myself wondering at being called everyone's 'Dear!' " Yes, these are stock phrases, but they express at least a surface sense of connection, a bit of attention thrown one's way. When I'm checking out groceries at the supermarket, I always say, "Thank you." to the person bagging the groceries, and they inevitably respond with, "Have a nice day." In the smallest of ways we have acknowledged the reality of one another's presence, and this is a tiny exchange of kind speech, however formulaic.

We gain pleasure from using kind speech because we see its effect reflected in others' pleasure. I think there is also a deep-seated pleasure when we use Right Speech in its meanings of true, correct, and beneficial. We sense its "rightness" as an acknowledgment of the truths of impermanence and interdependence, the Right View that forms the foundation for the entire Eightfold Path. Following this Path eases our struggles and quiets our anxieties because, by so doing, we live a life illuminated by our understanding and acceptance of the truth of impermanence and interdependence. With this understanding, we become flexible and live the elements of the Eightfold Path in acceptance of constant change—the ceaseless alteration of the context within which we are bound, not only to all other living beings, but also to the objects we encounter. With acceptance comes the delight of no longer being alienated, separate, and out of control. Now we are included! We are no longer merely separate little drops of water. Now we move with the flow of the mighty stream of life. For me, the fact that I am included in this universe, that I belong, that I am important to it, is a source of endless wonder and gratitude. It is natural for me to have sympathy with other beings since we are rowing this boat together. We all belong. On the Path, it is natural that I try to find speech that is appropriate and beneficial, for it is being offered to my companions.

This is not to say that Right Speech comes easily. From our investigation of Right Speech thus far, it is easy to see that there are complex nuances of which I must be aware. It is also clear that my own perceptions may be flawed. To accomplish Right Speech, at least some of the time, I must pay particular attention to Right View along with the other "Right" steps on the path. Can I be completely certain that what I say is true, kind, and appropriate to this moment? In reality, no, I cannot.

It is important to remember that another component of the Path is Right Effort. In her introduction, Byakuren placed Right Effort at the center of her chart of the relationship between the elements of the Eightfold Path with the notation "not too tight, not too loose." As we walk the Eightfold Path, we may find it full of potholes or discover that it leads up steep hills and abruptly drops into valleys. Sometimes we can see where we are going; sometimes we walk blindly. What we must not do is turn the Eightfold Path into an unrealistic goal, a picture of unattainable perfection. If we do that, we deny the promise of the Third Noble Truth and merely act out once more the struggles of the Second Noble Truth to control and attain. When we grasp at perfection, our struggle to meet an impossible goal will lead us back to *dukkha*, the First Noble Truth of suffering.

We hold firm to our intention to have our speech and our gestures realize Right Speech, yet we know that it is hopeless to struggle and strain toward perfection. It is not in accord with the two great truths of impermanence and interdependence to think there is some perfect Speech out there that we may attain and never again find ourselves uttering a word out of tune with the situation. It is as hopeless as yearning to be forever young; but we can point ourselves in the direction of truth and compassion in our speech and learn from our mistakes. We can be aware of what it means to open our mouth and form words. As the Buddha admonishes us in the *Samyutta Nikaya*, we can abstain from false, malicious, and harsh speech and avoid idle chatter.

In this latter context, let us remind ourselves that, at times, a companionable silence is preferable to a flood of pointless words. We chatter to assert our presence, to feel that we are alive, yet without real meaning the words lose their impact and roll off our ears without making the connection we so eagerly seek. A few days before writing this, I sat in an airport restaurant next to a group of five people who were chattering loudly and filling the room with noise. However, none of it had substance, and I realized soon that they were not really listening to one another and merely uttering words to shout "I am here!" Right Speech comes, not from self-assertion, but from a self open to real communication with others.

Another component of Right Speech, in addition to Right Silence, is Right Hearing. This may be the most difficult thing of all. We can, perhaps, learn to stop ourselves from blurting out hurtful, untrue, or inane words, but we hear the words of others as filtered through our ego and tainted by our delusions about our self. How often do misunderstandings arise because we have misconstrued something said? I may hear a comment about myself and interpret it as an attack, when the person actually meant it as a compliment, but it is out of sync with my self view, or perhaps I feel that the speaker has not presented an accurate picture.

Even more difficult is hearing the meaning beneath the words. To do so, we must be able to perceive that the speaker either does not mean what she has said, or that she has been fed a viewpoint that she's adopted thoughtlessly. The degree to which we can hear beyond and beneath words is the degree to which our compassion can be activated.

For example, in 1969 I found myself separated from my husband, living in a walk-up tenement in East Dedham, Massachusetts, raising two latch-key sons, at that time roughly ten and twelve years of age, and struggling to manage and sustain an avant-garde professional theatre company in Boston. Needless to say, I was exhausted and depressed most of the time. One morning, the boys seemed impossibly slow at getting ready and off to school in time, and I simply exploded, screaming at them to "Get out, get out! I hate you!" They slunk off to school and I went to the theatre, where the guilt over my behavior began to rise until it nearly swamped me. To make matters worse, there was some crisis at the theatre, and I had to make that awful call home to tell them I wouldn't be home for supper, but there were a couple of hot dogs in the fridge. (We were subsisting on less than welfare at that time.)

I finally stumbled up the steps to our apartment about ten o'clock. I have never forgotten what I found: from the single light bulb in the living room hung three balloons and on the coffee table were three bottles of Coke. A shirt cardboard also hung from the light fixture, and on it was awkwardly printed: "We love you all the tine [sic] and don't forget it." "We thought you needed a party," said one of the boys. The gratitude I felt that night will remain with me always. They had heard my misery below the hateful words that I'd spoken.

I spoke earlier about the problem of the ego's intrusion into what we say and what we hear. The Buddha's teaching of "no-self," or no fixed and permanent entity we can call the self, becomes clear when we think of this self as the product of causes and effects, and of relationships with others, all of which are subject to incessant change. From this viewpoint, it may seem "right" to think of our speech as issuing from a place of selflessness, but this, too, is an area in which we must be cautious. In our desire to accomplish Right Speech, we may speak from a place of self-abnegation that is not helpful. To speak self-deprecatingly is actually an attempt to use servile speech as a means of accomplishing our ends. We seek to enhance our self-esteem or advance toward our goal by currying the approval of others, although we often merely arouse their contempt, for they see through our servile words.

In *Bodaisatta-shishobo*, the first of the four elements of a bodhisattva's activity to lead others to liberation is "free giving," and I think it relates to what I have just said about manipulative speech. Dogen says: " 'Free giving' means not being greedy. Not being greedy means not coveting. Not coveting means, in everyday language, not courting favor (Nishijima and Cross 3:29)." Servile speech may be flattery, but it lacks the necessary element of truth.

Speech can also be utilized as a barrier to those who are not "ours," rather than as a way to open communication between us. Specialized jargon has this effect. An example within Buddhism is using too many references to Sanskrit words that put off the everyday listener. Other forms of exclusionary language can be found in the deliberate use of multisyllabic words to show off one's education, when words of one syllable might well suffice. Regional slang, "Black English," and coded gang speech are other examples. This speech is meant only for those in the inner circle.

We can also be arrogant about our ability to use our own language and fail to appreciate the frustration of those struggling to express themselves in a new language. When I am in Japan and can barely speak at the level of a three-year-old, my frustration can rise to the boiling point, and I want to shout, "I can express difficult concepts in English!"

Additionally, we can use a person's struggle with our language as an excuse to look down on them. Some years ago, I was in Chicago for some kind of meeting, went out to dinner, and took a cab back to the hotel. I noticed the cab driver, probably hailing from some part of the Indian subcontinent, had a children's book propped up on the dashboard of the cab. When I asked him if he was learning English, he grinned and said, "Yes. I learn just as children do." Then he told me that he'd been in the U.S. a relatively brief time, but that he'd worked in some capacity with an American firm in India. He mentioned that the American employees had laughed at him and teased him about his poor English. "So now," he said proudly, "I add English to Hindi, Urdu, and four regional dialects." He was proudly multilingual but had been disrespected because he was not a member of the exclusive club of English speakers. I asked him to teach me the Urdu word for "thank you" and to the amazement of the hotel doorman, I leaped from the cab gaily saying "thank you" in Urdu. I no longer remember the word, but the lesson about not judging others by their proficiency or lack thereof in my native language has stuck with me all these years.

I mentioned earlier that our demeanor, our stance, our gesture are also forms of speech. Each thing eloquently expresses itself directly, as it is. There was a famous controversy in China in the centuries preceding the life of Dongshan Lianjie (807-869; Jpn.: Tozan Ryokai). The question was whether non-sentient beings could expound dharma. At the heart of this was the issue of whether dharma consisted solely of the words of the Buddha and other great teachers or should be understood more broadly as an expression of the immanent reality of all things, sentient and non-sentient alike.

There is a story about Dongshan in *Just This Is It*, by Taigen Dan Leighton (20-26), that illustrates the speaking of the non-sentient. Dongshan relates to National Teacher Guishan Lingyou (771-853; Jpn.: Isan Reiyu) a story he had heard about a student who questioned National Teacher Nanyang Huizhong (Jpn.: Nan'yo Echu) as to whether non-sentient beings expound the dharma. Huizhong answered that they did so incessantly and quoted a scriptural source, the *Avatamsaka Sutra*, which states: "The earth expounds Dharma, living beings expound it, throughout the three times, everything expounds it."

When asked to comment, Guishan raised his flywhisk. Dongshan did not understand and Guishan suggested that he take his question to Yunyan. Dongshan asked Yunyan who can hear the non-sentient expound the dharma and Yunyan said the non-sentient hear it. Again, Dongshan did not understand when Yunyan raised his flywhisk in demonstration. Yunyan also gave Dongshan a verse to contemplate, this time from the Pure Land *Amitabha Sutra*: "Water birds, tree groves, all without exception recite the Buddha's name, recite the Dharma." Dongshan reflected on this and composed a verse:

> How marvelous! How marvelous!
> The Dharma expounded by nonsentient beings is inconceivable.
> Listening with your ears, no sound.
> Hearing with your eyes, you directly understand. (Powell 26)

The speech of inanimate things (non-sentient beings) is not in words but in their form itself. A tree speaks the Dharma of a tree, a bird of a bird, and if we listen with our eyes, indeed with all our senses, we will hear that Dharma as clearly as those Parisians read my stance and walk as shouting "American!" What's more, the Dharma that the non-sentient expound so thoroughly is that of impermanence and interdependence.

The Eightfold Path offers us a road map for an enlightened life. The *Avatamsaka Sutra* traces the career of great enlightening beings on their path to Buddhahood and as an inspiration for us sets forth the kind of speech exercised by these bodhisattvas.

> Great enlightening beings have ten kinds of speech: gentle speech, causing all sentient beings to be calm; sweet elixir speech, caus-

ing all sentient beings to be clear and cool; nondeceptive speech, everything they say being true; truthful speech, not lying even in dreams; great speech, being honored by all the gods; profound speech, revealing the essence of things; steadfast speech, expounding truth inexhaustibly; straightforward speech, their statements being easy to understand; various speech being spoken according to the occasion; speech enlightening all sentient beings, enabling them to understand according to their inclinations. Based on these, enlightening beings attain the supreme subtle speech of buddhas. (Cleary 1069)

We've considered multiple facets of Right Speech, so it may seem complicated, and we wonder, "How am I going to keep all that in mind?" We should take comfort in awareness that the Path is paved with words said in truth and in kindness by beings as ordinary and fallible as we. Feeling deep gratitude that this moment is now our opportunity, we add our words and our kindness.

Let us close by returning to the Buddha's very practical instructions as spoken in the *Abhayarajakumara Sutta*:

So, too, prince, such speech as the Tathagata knows to be untrue, incorrect and unbeneficial, and which is also unwelcome and disagreeable to others: such speech the Tathagata does not utter. Such speech as the Tathagata knows to be true and correct but unbeneficial, and which is also unwelcome and disagreeable to others: such speech the Tathagata does not utter. Such speech as the Tathagata knows to be true, correct, and beneficial, but which is unwelcome and disagreeable to others, the Tathagata knows the time to use such speech. Such speech as the Tathagata knows to be untrue, incorrect and unbeneficial, but which is welcome and agreeable to others, such speech the Tathagata does not utter. Such speech as the Tathagata knows to be true and correct but unbeneficial, and which is welcome and agreeable to others, such speech the Tathagata does not utter. Such speech as the Tathagata knows to be true, correct and beneficial, and which is welcome and agreeable to others: the Tathagata knows the time to use such speech. Why is that? Because the Tathagata has compassion for beings. (Nanamoli and Bodhi 500)

The Buddha laid out the Eightfold Path as a blueprint for a life lived in joyous acceptance of the changing nature of this life and the manner in which all things are bound together in a mutual dance of interdependent existence. Our acceptance of the invitation to walk this Path is the beginning of our true life.

Let us approach with joy the opportunity to speak appropriately, fully aware, and offer wisdom, perception, and kindness as best we can as we embrace the Buddha's Right Speech as part of our Path to liberation for our self and others.

Works cited

Bodhi, Bhikkhu, trans. *The Connected Discourses of the Buddha: A New Translation of the Samyutta Nikaya*. 2 vols. Boston: Wisdom, 2000.

Cleary, Thomas, trans. *The Flower Ornament Scripture: A Translation of the Avatamsaka Sutra*. Boston: Shambala, 1993.

Dogen, Eihei. "Bodaisatta-shishobo (Four Elements of a Bodhisattva's Social Relations)." *Master Dogen's Shobogenzo*. Trans. Gudo Nishijima and Chodo Cross. 4 vols. London: Windbell, 1997.

Leighton, Taigen Dan. *Just This Is It: Dongshan and the Practice of Suchness*. Boston: Shambhala, 2015.

Liang-chieh. *The Record of Tung-shan*. William Powell, trans. Honolulu: Univ of Hawai'i Press, 1986.

Nanamoli, Bhikkhu, trans. "Kalama Sutta." *The Life of the Buddha: According to the Pali Canon*. Sri Lanka: First BPS Pariyatti Edition, 2001.

Nanamoli, Bhikkhu and Bhikkhu Bodhi, trans. "Abhayarajakumara Sutta (The Discourse to Prince Abhaya)." *The Middle Length Discourses of the Buddha: A Translation of the Majjhima Nikaya*. Boston: Wisdom, 2015.

Powell, William, trans. *Record of Tung-shan*. Honolulu: U of Hawaii Press, 1986.

Chapter 4

Right Action: The World Is My Body
Shodo Spring

It was my first sesshin. "Innumerable labors have brought us this food. We should know how it comes to us." A one-day retreat, and I encountered the meal chant for the first time. "As we receive this offering, we should consider whether our virtue and practice deserve it." During the break, I grabbed a chant book and started to memorize, fully aware of the no-reading rules.

> As we desire the natural condition of mind, to be free from cling-ing we must be free from greed. To support our life we take this food. To attain the Buddha Way we take this food. This food is for the Three Treasures, for our parents, teachers, leaders and home-land, and for all beings in the six worlds. Thus we eat this food with everyone. We eat to end all evil, to practice good, to save all sentient beings, and to accomplish the Buddha Way. (Minnesota Zen Meditation Center chant book)

This old translation spoke to me so deeply, uncorrected, naming our place within the whole cycle of things. "Innumerable labors": Not only the cook, the kitchen helper, the grocery store clerk, truck drivers, and farmworkers, but the plants, the soil microbes and fungi, worms and beetles, compost and manure, weeds that bring the minerals up from the depths, wind and rain and sun—a whole world of beings works and plays together, and somehow comes to me through the food that grows thus. Even if I grow my own food, as I do, if I compost local plant and animal manures, terrace the garden so it holds the water straight from the sky, plant every seed with my own hands, say a blessing over each one, watch it and weed it, mulch and tend it and then harvest, clean, and prepare it with great effort—even then, the innumerable labors are way beyond this individual self. Life is a gift. "Whether our virtue and practice deserve it?" There is no such thing as deserving this gift. To be alive is a gift, freely given by the world around us, which does not judge or censure us. How does one live? What response can possibly be appropriate for a gift of such magnitude?

We receive food simply to support life. We receive food so that we can practice the Buddha Way. We receive food, first for the Three Treasures—Buddha, Dharma, and Sangha. Perhaps Sangha includes family, community, society, culture, and bodhisattvas. In Japanese, "*Ho*" or "Dharma" can mean law, rule, morality, method/system/process, art, religion, or doctrine. I can only believe it includes biochemical processes as well as the structures of karma and the way the whole universe works. Surely Buddha includes the vast sky, the body of the universe beyond our ability to imagine. How could the Three Treasures be limited to what our minds can know?

We also receive food on behalf of the four benefactors, here named as: parents, who gave us life and early training; teachers, who offer the Dharma, who guide and support us in the Way; worldly leaders who take care of the mundane world; homeland, the culture that shaped us and/or the myriad living beings and nonliving things that nourished us. The list only mentions humans, but surely it includes others sentient and non-sentient: minerals, water, air, electrons, microbes, bugs, worms, plants, and other beings.

We receive food for all beings, no exceptions, and thus we also receive food along with everyone. We are part of this crowd of life. Our intention is to end all evil, to practice good, to free beings, and to accomplish the Way.

Right Action is like this. It arises, simply and directly, from understanding our place in the world—the understanding that we call Right View. When there is nothing but the gift, what can there be but gratitude? When there is nothing but gratitude, what arises will naturally be what we call Right Action. There is no need for control or even a decision on our part. And, because we are part of the whole throng of living beings, Right Action is action on behalf of those beings and on behalf of the Way that sustains us.

THE GROUND OF RIGHT ACTION
The Buddha's Compassion

In *Returning To Silence*, Katagiri Roshi spoke about the compassion of the Buddha's world:

> All sentient beings are allowed to live and are, from the be-
> ginning, forgiven for living their lives in this world. Everything,
> whatever it is, has some reason why it exists: evil, good, even some-
> thing neither evil nor good. You cannot destroy devils just because
> you don't like them. Even though you don't like monsters, still
> there is some reason why they exist. Everything is entitled to live
> in this world in peace and harmony beyond our judgment, our
> evaluation. This is the first condition we have to realize—every-
> thing is buddha. (73)

As I consider this matter of being forgiven, a softness arises. The voices of internal critics hush for a moment. Sentient beings are "forgiven for living their lives in this world." I am included, this sentient being, forgiven for living my life, for having emotions, actions, and impacts, for taking space, for using air, water, and food that might be better spent elsewhere. No, it wouldn't be better spent elsewhere. I'm welcome here, belonging, forgiven, embraced. If I were gone, the whole world would miss me, just as I miss my sister whose death left a hole in my life. This person, this sentient being, matters to the world around me. *What I do matters.* My actions create my own world and also the world of those around me, just as their actions create my world, just as everyone's actions together create the whole world.

Katagiri continues:

> The second condition we have to realize is that the self must
> readily accept the compassion of Buddha's world. . . . we must ac-
> tualize Buddha's compassion in our everyday lives. We have to live
> our lives in the complete realization that we are already forgiven,
> that we are already allowed to live, and that we, ourselves, must
> make our lives come alive. (73-74)

Our lives do not take place in our idea of the world or in our idea of ourselves. They occur in the middle of the Buddha's compassion, and to be alive we must completely realize that compassion. We create our own lives; we make ourselves alive, in the middle of a dynamic universe. The life of practice is not passive. It acts; it takes initiative. It reaches out to embrace the universe. The shape of that embrace is not prescribed, but embracing the universe is the nature of Right Action.

THE GROUND OF RIGHT ACTION
Right View

Most human beings operate from the imagination of separate existence, of myself as one who acts on other people, beings, and things who are seen as objects to be acted upon. It is in this imagination that we are able to talk about our actions, words, thoughts, and even our spiritual practice, as if they are something we "do." On the one hand, this is confusion, a mistaken view. On the other hand, it's hard to discuss these matters without stepping into a conceptual framework.

When I said before that "I" eat, "I" receive, "I" am given, those words are said within that framework, that convenience. Actually, on a physical basis, energy is transferred here and there around the physical world, and it moves among various points of consciousness that experience themselves as identities—human or otherwise. I have no direct experience of the consciousness that exists within the bird, the tree, or the microbe, and don't know whether these beings experience themselves as identities like I do, but I have heard about the vast communication networks within forests that send information and sometimes nourishment between trees via mycelial (fungal) networks spanning miles. I have heard that chickens dream. This leads me to feel less special as human, but vastly more secure, embraced by innumerable beings who support each other, who support all, which includes this one point of awareness, and all the points of awareness of any kind.

Here we are in relationship. Here we are, embraced by everything that lives—by the sun, wind and trees, by the air, mosquitoes and water, and by each being/thing we eat and that eats us—all of us together creating a world and created by the world. There is nothing but process, Indra's net. We see only the knots, the apparent individuals, but they are actually jewels—reflecting each other, creating self and other in unending creation, the dance of life and death. I am reminded of writer Daniel Quinn's phrase "living in the hands of the gods," and of the term "decolonize consciousness," used by the Evolver Network to denote a movement to abandon the archetype of humans as masters of an inert universe, reviving the way of relationship with all beings. It is not only Buddhists that understand Right View.

Of course, I use the word "I," along with words like "we" and "our" that refer to a self while acknowledging that a sense of self is illusory. The Japanese word for self "*ji*" pictures an eye with a pointer. Something looks out from this place. There is a point of consciousness—there are a million billion trillion points of consciousness—each looking out, each probably imagining itself to have a separate existence of some kind, each witnessing all the others and, by that witness, creating them. Would I write if you were not here to read? This momentary, instantaneous self, like a flash of lightning, also vanishes in a flash. It is created by all the other witnesses even as it helps to create all of them in the magnificent dance of interdependent co-arising. In the middle of this dance, saying "I" is merely a convenience so "we" can talk about "other" things.

GROUNDING RIGHT ACTION IN OUR LIVES
The Teachings

Right View might seem abstract, but Buddhism is full of teachings that can help us bring Right View into our own lives to inform Right Action.

Metta Sutta

The *Metta Sutta* or Loving Kindness Meditation advises us:

> Let one be strenuous, upright, and sincere, without pride, easily contented, and joyous. Let one not be submerged by the things of the world. Let one not take upon oneself the burden of riches. Let one's senses be controlled. Let one be wise but not puffed up and let one not desire great possessions even for one's family. Let one do nothing that is mean or that the wise would reprove. (SFZC, par. 2)

The life of the sincere practitioner—"one who seeks the good and has obtained peace"—is energetic and upright. The attitude is not obsession with things of the world such as money, possessions, fame, the accumulation of interesting experiences, nor even a thousand Twitter followers, a reputation as a sage, or successful sales of your Dharma book. We can use these instructions to see where we fall short and to advise our aspiration to uprightness. At the same time, this sutra also wishes happiness to all: "Whether weak or strong, in high or middle or low realms of existence, small or great, . . . may all beings be happy (par. 3)." Just as Katagiri Roshi observed that we are all forgiven for existing, the *Metta Sutta* wishes us happiness and safety no matter who we are, and offers guidance for Right Action:

> Let no one deceive another nor despise any being in any state. Let none by anger or hatred wish harm to another. Even as a mother at the risk of her life watches over and protects her only child, so with a boundless mind should one cherish all living things, suffusing love over the entire world, above, below, and all around, without limit, so let one cultivate an infinite good will toward the whole world. (par. 4)

Do not deceive and do not despise anyone, but cherish them as you would your own child. (Even cockroaches? Even kudzu? Even [insert name of favorite political villain here]? Yes, even them.) To be at peace, to do good, we cannot despise anyone.

Short story: Working in landscaping, I was asked to pull out euonymous, a local problem plant. I paid close attention as I pulled it out by the roots, trying to remove each single plant completely. Somehow, as this became my regular practice, there arose a quality of kindness. Eventually the thought of liberating the plants from their attachment and greed replaced the thought of eradicating them. I looked forward to the days of removing those very tenacious roots. All illusion, of course, but some illusions soften the heart while others harden it.

Another story: once in ceremony I walked over the land where I live, asking the trees and plants to support the spiritual and environmental work I wished to do to support them. It seemed to me that they answered yes. The longer I walked, the more I asked; finally I was asking support from the buckthorn, which I planned to tear out by the roots, and I imagined they too supported me. Now, when I tear out buckthorn, there is a sadness in it, yet I remove it, because like civilized humans, it cannot keep its place; it overtakes everything and kills without awareness. I don't despise it. I recognize it as kin, and I do not allow it to kill. (I would do the same for my own species, if I could find a way.) I carry on this practice even though it seems hopeless. I don't resort to chemicals, which destroy widely; I stay with the intimate practice of pulling up each individual, knowing what I have done. My intention is to do a larger good in caring for the land. Have I then appointed myself master of this place? Or am I simply one of its members, seeking what makes life good for me? Is this Right Action informed by Right Intention?

Let us acknowledge ourselves as animals who need food, water, warmth, shelter, and safety, and who desire comfort, love, and security. We are the top predators in this system. The necessity of the predator is to take care of its prey as a whole, or this predator will not survive. Survival is the necessity that civilized humans, including Buddhists, often forget. We forget we cannot survive without caring for the community of life. Thus, as a society that has replaced an ethic of community with the social value of self-interest, we find ourselves here in the Anthropocene, watching the Great Extinction of species, listening to reports of floods and fires (those of us who are not running from them), and arguing about whether technological capitalism will save us or destroy us all.

Let us remember that we are animals and our existence is precarious. Our existence has always been precarious, dependent on the whole community of beings in a very physical way. Let us forgive ourselves, as we are already forgiven, for being animals. Let us forgive ourselves for loving our own children more than those of others, as animals do. Like animals, trees, and humans, let us be willing to sacrifice this individual self for the sake of the whole.

Finally, here is the place where Right View arises: our tribe is not just our biological family, local community, or people who look like us. Our tribe is all sentient beings. The predator cares for the prey species for survival reasons. The awakened one cares for them because they are ourselves. "Standing or walking, sitting or lying down, during all one's waking hours, let one practice the way with gratitude (SFZC, par. 5)."

Three Pure Precepts

In the *Dhammapada* (the collected sayings of the Buddha) the Buddha says: "To avoid all evil, to cultivate good, and to cleanse one's mind—this is the teaching of the Buddhas (Buddharakkhita Dhp 183)." This earliest teaching of the precepts by the Buddha is straightforward, simple, and paradoxical. Cultivating good can be defined in an ordinary way, as can avoiding evil, but "cleansing your mind" does not mean to think only positive and kind thoughts, nor does it have other ordinary meanings. It is, fundamentally, Katagiri's first condition: "to realize that everything is

Buddha." It means to refrain from dualism, renouncing thoughts of good and evil. Without thoughts of good and evil, how does Right Action arise? Without imagining evil, how can we avoid it?

Zen's Three Pure Precepts offer a possible resolution. The translation I like best comes from the Ancient Dragon Zen Gate temple in Chicago. It reads: "I vow to embrace and sustain right conduct. I vow to embrace and sustain all good. I vow to embrace and sustain all beings." We vow to enter a relationship, a relationship that is both intimate (embrace) and active (sustain). Vowing to sustain right conduct, we commit ourselves to ethical behavior as part of the community that supports and sustains us in practice. Vowing to sustain all good, we make it our business to be involved. Vowing to sustain all beings, we are inexorably drawn into relationship: with the victims of war (and its perpetrators); with animals going extinct, floods and droughts, forest fires and the innumerable beings that die in them; with child slaves and their overseers; with homeless people and the one percent; with terrorists, capitalists, communists, and revolutionaries of all stripes; and with people who just want to be left alone. We also are compelled to enter relationship with the cause of the suffering we see around us. That cause? Say hello to the Three Poisons. We meet greed, anger, and delusion with kindness—not to eradicate them, nor to be ruled by them, but to live with them like one might live with a difficult sibling.

The Three Pure Precepts ground us in relationship, which supports and sustains Right Action.

Three Minds

What is the result of living, not as an "individual," but as relationship, abandoning the illusion of separation? What, exactly, is the Right Action of embracing all beings? One way of describing it is Uchiyama Roshi's teaching of the Three Minds in *Opening the Hand of Thought*. These are joyful mind, magnanimous mind and nurturing mind (127-137).

Magnanimous mind or big mind embraces the whole, not a part. It has the stability and spaciousness of the ocean rather than the movement of the wave. It accepts and welcomes all beings and all events with equanimity. When asked "How shall we treat others?" big mind says with Ramana Maharshi, "There are no others."

Joyful mind arises when the barriers of separation drop away and one finds oneself in the middle of all beings, celebrated, receiving and giving freely, abundantly and fully living within a brilliant vibrant universe, in dance, rejoicing, song, and celebration.

Nurturing mind, literally "old woman mind," is like the mind or heart of a grandmother's love for her grandchildren, extending everywhere. The archetype of grandmother is unconditional love: inspiring respect, offering wisdom, and most of all, kindness with loving presence. We are encouraged to love, not to control.

Of course, we want to remember that the Japanese word we translate as "mind" also means "heart," and the character is a picture of a heart. When you ask a Japanese person to point to their mind, they point to a place in the middle of their chest, so we remember that these three minds are not only intellectual, not cognitive, but rather indicate an attitude, a way of being. When we access the Three Minds to support Right Action, life becomes joyful, spacious, and nurturing. Embraced within life, our hearts become joyful, spacious, and nurturing, and our actions are influenced by this expansion.

Ten Grave Precepts

> To study the Buddha Way is to study the self. To study the self is to forget the self. To forget the self is to be verified by all things. To be verified by all things is to let the body and mind of the self and the body and mind of others drop off. There is a trace of realization that cannot be grasped. We endlessly express this ungraspable trace of realization. (Okumura 2)

Right Action is something that arises naturally from living in the context of the compassionate functioning of the whole. It arises when the self slips away—falls away so completely that you cannot find even a trace of realization. Nevertheless, there is expression. Without thought, without an idea of self, but realized, verified, witnessed, and created by all beings, expression arises, completely filling life. There is Right Action.

And for the rest of us? For ordinary unrealized sentient beings filled with ideas of self and other, besieged with preferences—where is Right Action for us? I heard this quotation years ago, in the hallways at Minnesota Zen Center: "The Precepts are the one cause of the Zen gate." Care for our conduct, our action, our morality is the cause of passing through that mythical gate of realization where fish become dragons, the cause of being transformed from illusory separate being to the speck on the wave of the universe. How is this? Calm the actions and the mind follows. Refrain from hateful speech. Don't hit, don't steal, don't lie, don't indulge in intoxicants, don't slander, don't create divisiveness—every harmful action not taken opens space to forget the self, and thus to be verified by all things. Changing our actions changes our thoughts, and from calming thought Right Action arises.

Even though on an absolute level there is no "me" and no "doing," what, in this world of beings, things, and doing, shall I do? As Dogen says: "Our lifespan is too short to waste a moment . . . Our body and mind are like equipment in the common area [of the monastery] (Tanahashi 685)." This body/mind is like equipment for all to use, and this use happens in a context as sacred as a monastery. Once we have entered this context (through receiving the precepts, in particular), our actions are not personal but are responses in service to the whole. Our actions are ceremony, the smallest movement a sacred liturgy influencing the working of everything. The expression goes on forever, unlimited in time and space, ungraspable.

RIGHT ACTION IN CONTEXT

Sangha

Sangha means group, organization, or gathering in Sanskrit. In Buddhism, it refers to the Buddhist community—sometimes only the monastic community, sometimes all practitioners, and occasionally referring to all beings as "*sangha.*"

It matters to be part of a sangha. Of course, community is the natural state of humans, which is one reason to participate in it. There are other reasons. Many people begin their practice by reading books, figuring out how to sit by themselves, perhaps traveling to hear a teacher, but then returning to practice alone. Some of the "benefits" of sangha include not feeling alone, having to look at why you still feel alone when surrounded by community, having people to correct you when you get confused, and especially getting called out when you become proud of your learning or your practice. Having to deal with difficult people in a setting of practice—for instance, your work supervisor gives confusing instructions and then criticizes your mistakes—is a chance to watch how anger arises in your own body-mind, because a practice setting supports examination rather than judgment.

However, accepting strict teaching should not be confused with complete passivity. I can remember occasions when my attempts to avoid challenging authority meant that, by not acting, I allowed harm to happen. Allowing even small harms to occur in a sangha can evolve into allowing large harms. Questions must be asked with care and attention. What is Right Action in this situation? Actions that look like abuse of authority must be questioned, challenged, and perhaps even discussed by the whole sangha. That questioning is a place of practice. For the one who holds a position of authority in sangha, Right Action means it is essential to be careful of one's personal actions while supporting a sangha climate that encourages these questions.

Public Engagement

A fragment of a poem by Warshan Shire has been going around Facebook since the Paris bombing in November 2015. It seems worth mentioning that the poem starts with: "They set my aunt's house on fire."

What They Did Yesterday Afternoon
...i've been praying,
and these are what my prayers look like;
dear god
i come from two countries
one is thirsty
the other is on fire
both need water.
later that night
i held an atlas in my lap
ran my fingers across the whole world
and whispered
where does it hurt?
it answered
everywhere
everywhere
everywhere. (Shire para 2-4)

Life contains suffering.

We must consider some difficult things here. The hope is to allow some gentleness around them, making it easier to think and talk about the hard subjects of our life today. I'm thinking about war, torture, racism and colonialism; terrorism; pollution, climate change, and hunger;

corporate greed and power; governmental corruption; and some responses to these. I'm thinking about two African and four Central American indigenous environmental activists shot in a single three-week period, about having more than one presidential candidate openly promoting hate.

What is Right Action in this context? The Buddhist world is sharply divided about engagement in public life or political action. On the one hand, is it not my first responsibility to calm the mind, to become free from suffering and carry others across to peace and freedom? On the other hand, how can I pretend to be separate from everything around me? All beings create me, moment by moment; how can I ignore them when they are suffering? Still, wouldn't the most useful thing be to offer them the Dharma? The argument goes around and around in circles.

Luca Valentino writes: "How we act, what we do, and how we think and decide creates the world we experience and the experiences of those who encounter us. We cannot escape or avoid the consequences of our actions and the thoughts that lie behind our actions. Our thoughts drive our actions and our actions drive our lives (personal email)."

The world comes in layers. In the ultimate, everything is peace, and it's fair to say everything else we experience is delusion. In the dependently-arisen world, the one where everything is constantly creating everything else, this momentary illusory individual makes a contribution to the entire working of the world around us. What kind of contribution shall we make? What is our gift, our offering?

Last November, an hour from my own home, Minneapolis police shot an unarmed young Black man. The news was nearly drowned out by the news of a terrorist attack in Paris, another the day before in Beirut, and uncountable acts that year in places such as Kenya, Palestine, *everywhere*. I cannot count. A week after the Minneapolis shooting, protesters were still camped out by the local police station. If there had been no public response to the shooting, this death would have disappeared. Some kinds of action could have created division and more suffering. The protestors seemed to walk a middle path, demanding change without violent action.

I had to make a decision. What was Right Action in this situation? I visited the protestors twice, a few hours each time, brought food and warm clothes, and once helped with cleanup. I posted some reports online because media coverage seemed a little biased. The protestors' response evolved day by day, without plans. The question I asked myself was whether my body in that place would be more useful than the other things I was doing at home.

Zen master Yunmen was once asked: "What are the teachings of a whole lifetime?" Yunmen answered: "An appropriate statement (Cleary and Cleary 94)." When suffering arises, we always have to decide what to do. That's not quite right. We have to get out of the way and let appropriate action arise, but usually we call that deciding.

In a YouTube presentation, Derrick Jensen, a non-Buddhist environmentalist, offers five questions that can clarify the direction and scope of an appropriate statement. "What do you love? What are your gifts? What is the largest, most pressing problem that you can help to solve using the gifts that are unique to you in all the universe? What does your landbase need to survive?" and finally the direct, "Are you going to do it?" (Jensen 2012). The question is not what large flashy thing you should do about a currently popular issue; it's what Right Action you can take to make an appropriate statement.

The World

In *Love in Action*, Thich Nhat Hanh writes from the heart of the Vietnam war. His message is directed toward those inclined to active engagement.

> The nature of the struggle is not a doctrine to be materialized by a program of action; it is communication and love. Thus, its leaders must create and inspire love for the masses in the hearts of their people. They touch the people by altruistic acts born from their own love. When Nhat Chi Mai burned herself because she wanted to be a "torch in the dark night," she moved millions of Vietnamese. The force she engendered was the force of love for non-violent action. (Nhat Hahn)

Are you horrified? I was when the first Buddhist monk burned himself during the Vietnam war. All I could think of was how painful it must have been. Later I learned of the long Asian tradition of "making oneself into a candle" as an offering. These monks and nuns merely turned that tradition into a means of public communication.

After the Paris attacks in November 2015, I received a list of terrorist assaults, compiled by a Facebook friend, which listed thirteen attacks from various sources within the past seventy-two days that caused ten to 224 deaths per attack. This list did not include the ongoing trauma in Palestine, nor deaths from floods, drought, earthquake, and oil and natural gas explosions. In all of these incidents, we did not count the nonhuman dead, the dozens of species that go extinct each day in the human-caused Sixth Mass Extinction. Then there are the immediate stories such as the Minneapolis killing noted before, in addition to every individual instance of murder, rape, or abuse.

Two states in the U.S. responded to the Paris attacks by saying they would refuse immigration from Muslims, or from Syrian refugees—no, three states, no, twenty-one states, no, thirty-one states and the House of Representatives. France responded with a bombing raid and draconian security measures. Meanwhile, unnoticed, a mining disaster in Brazil killed nine and destroyed a whole village. Meanwhile, the planet moved ever faster toward unstoppable climate change, with effects already ranging from higher food prices to famine, death, refugees, and wars. This rolling disaster seems unstoppable because, apparently, "the economy" and profit are nonnegotiable, even in the face of current disaster, even when the lives of our own children are at stake.

The world seems to have gone insane.

This world is my body. When my body is on fire, how do I take care of it? Jump into a tub of water, yes. When my body is on fire with hate, killing, greed, lies, where is there a tub of water large enough to immerse the world? Is there an ocean of love? Or a vast cool sky of equanimity? What is Right Action within this maelstrom? Perhaps a billion people sitting zazen around the clock would cool the world, or a billion people meditating on loving-kindness or chanting. "Hatred never ceases with hatred, by love alone it is healed. This is an ancient and eternal law." The Buddha's words from the *Dhammapada* gave peace in the Cambodian refugee camps once; I've found Americans respond to them as well. What if we all agreed to meditate or chant, perhaps in relays, until change happens? What if? Walk. Pray. Fast. I know people who are preparing to fight with guns, if it becomes necessary. Although I find that a bad idea in numberless ways, I cannot guarantee there will never be an appropriate situation for such a response.

Finding "an appropriate statement" may take a whole lifetime. Actually, I don't think we find it. I think we allow Right Action to come forth, having prepared the ground through practice and meditation.

Once, I thought I had found an appropriate statement in response to climate change and corporate irresponsibility, or I should say I thought that statement had found me. As I sat in the zendo during a three-month training period, visions of walking along the proposed Keystone XL pipeline route began to appear. It seemed possible that this vision might be something to act out. I sought counsel with teachers, and I continued to practice with the community. As the outer voices matched the inner voice, as the vision became clearer, commitment gradually became certain. When, months later, a Dharma sister noted how busy I was and asked "What if you didn't do the Walk?" my reply was clear: "For the rest of my life I would have wondered what would have happened if I did it."

I'd been studying "appropriate statement" for a few years by then. It began, really, when at the age of fifty-five, torn between monastic practice and activism, I sat zazen in public outside of the political conventions of both parties. To get from one convention to the other, I joined a month-long group walk called the DNC2RNC. What happened is not so important. What matters now is that I learned the experience of following the inner direction—learned it with my body and mind.

So when I felt called to walk along the KXL, I said yes. The walk was difficult and uncomfortable; sometimes it was scary. I made many mistakes and was too often angry, but there was never a question about doing it. I became familiar with the power of commitment. If there is one thing I would share from that experience, it is this: to be fully alive is to accept the work that comes to you right now, regardless of how big or small that work appears to be. I call that Right Action. And there is no way for me to know what that is for you.

The Whole Earth Is My Body

As Katagiri Roshi said: "Everything is buddha." In the ground of the Buddha's compassion, the whole world arises. Receiving the Buddha's compassion, acknowledging ourselves to be forgiven and allowing ourselves to be exactly who we are, we come to realize ever more deeply how we belong to this world. The entire world without exception really is the true human body, as Dogen said, and if we allow ourselves to meet it we are "verified by all things."

When the wisdom of Right View informs Right Action, we are fundamentally unable to act from greed, self-promotion, hate, revenge, and so forth. We are unable to act from delusion, the wish to escape, addiction, or craving, because those impulses are gone. To the extent that wisdom is present, the impetus toward harmful action disappears, and Right Action arises naturally.

Compassionate action can arise from our wish to be a certain kind of person, or even from our wish to be seen by others as a certain kind of person. Or, kind action can arise from our awareness of the nature of things: this sick person, that needy one, the polluted river, the endangered animal, the perpetrator and victim of harm—all are none other than my self. There is no separation.

Right Action comes from that place.

Works cited

"About us." *Evolver.* Evolver Holdings, Corp. 2016. Web. 19 Apr. 2016. <http://www.evolver.net/pages/about-us>.

Buddharakkhita, Archarya, trans. "Buddhavagga: The Buddha." *Access to Insight (Legacy Edition).* 30 Nov. 2013. Web. <http://www.accesstoinsight.org/tipitaka/kn/dhp/dhp.14.budd.html>.

Chant Book. Minnesota Zen Meditation Center, 1985.

Cleary, Thomas and J. C. Cleary, trans. *The Blue Cliff Record.* Boston: Shambhala, 1992.

Jensen, Derrick. "Derrick Jensen's Five Questions." YouTube. 31 Jan. 2012. Web. <https://www.youtube.com/watch?v=FjnS6WUFVLM>.

"Jukai" in "Sangha News." *Ancient Dragon Zen Gate.* Ancient Dragon Zen Gate, 2005-2016. Web. June 2012. <http://www.ancientdragon.org>

"Loving Kindness Meditation." *Teachings.* San Francisco Zen Center, 2016. Web. <http://www.sfzc.org/teachings/services-sutras-texts-songs>.

Katagiri, Dainin. *Returning to Silence: Zen Practice in Everyday Life.* Boston: Shambhala, 1988.

Nhat Hanh, Thich. *Love in Action: The Nonviolent Struggle for Peace in Vietnam.* Booklet. Paris: Vietnamese Buddhist Peace Delegation, 1969.

Okumura, Shohaku. *Realizing Genjokoan: The Key to Dogen's Shobogenzo.* Somerville, MA: Wisdom, 2010.

Quinn, Daniel. *Ishmael: An Adventure of the Mind and Spirit.* New York: Bantam/Turner, 1992.

Shire, Warshan. "What They Did Yesterday Afternoon." *poetry: once a day.* Wordpress.com. 28 Apr. 2015. Web. 28 May 2016. <https://poetrying.word-press.com/2015/04/28/what-they-did-yesterday-afternoon-warsan-shire/>.

Uchiyama, Kosho. *Opening the Hand of Thought: Foundations of Zen Buddhist Practice.* Trans. Tom Wright, Jisho Warner, and Shohaku Okumura. Somerville, MA: Wisdom, 2004.

Valentino, Luca. "Karma in Simple Language." Email to author. 28 Oct. 2015.

CHAPTER 5

Right Livelihood: Work as Spiritual Practice

By Misha Shungen Merrill

From the earliest days of my Buddhist practice, the Eightfold Path has been a touchstone of pragmatic wisdom for me. In particular, Right Livelihood always seemed to me to be of singular importance as a fundamental guide for anyone working in the modern world, but perhaps especially for someone like me: a lay person who wished to have a serious meditation practice but who, due to pre-existing responsibilities and obligations, needed to work in the marketplace and live a householder's life. How could I do this practice in an integrated and harmonious way?

I was fortunate that my Zen teacher, Les Keido Kaye, had already paved the way for someone in my position. Suzuki Roshi, the founder of the San Francisco Zen Center, agreed to ordain Les as a monk in the early 1970s, an unusual decision on his part given that Les was working full-time at IBM and had a family to support. Rather than leaving his family or his work to pursue meditation practice (as many of his contemporaries were doing), Les created a new path with Suzuki Roshi's blessing: a serious meditation practice based on monastic training, but designed for a lay community immersed in their jobs, families, mortgages, and the other accoutrements of worldly life. While those around him were leaving the marketplace behind and heading for the monastery, Les chose to practice right in the middle of the corporate world and use it as his training monastery.

Most of us are taught early in our lives to make a definite distinction between spiritual pursuits and ordinary life. In my case, I went to church on Sundays and attended a Catholic education class one day a week. The rest of the time life went on as usual with school, chores, and family dinners that seemed to have little relationship to the homilies being taught from the pulpit. Given this early disconnection between our religious training and the rest of our lives, most people choose one path or the other as adults—we either go away from the world into some monastic environment for spiritual training or we immerse ourselves in the everyday world of material needs and desires, "visiting" our spiritual life for an hour or so a week. To integrate both paths, however, is to understand the fundamental interconnectedness of our lives where Right View and Right Livelihood intersect. It is a manifestation of the Buddha's Middle Way in which everything from meditation to the family bank account offers a seamless practice opportunity. As Zen teacher, Ezra Bayda, writes in *Being Zen*: "Our real job—our life job . . . is to become awake to who we really are. When we remember this, we will be less likely to separate our work from our practice (98)."

It is no coincidence that the Buddha gave Right Livelihood the same weight and importance as Right View and Right Meditation in the Eightfold Path. In Western society, work is often seen as a kind of necessary evil that must be performed in order to afford the luxury of leisure or spiritual practice. When we have this attitude about work, we will naturally fall into the mistake of demeaning or elevating different kinds of work, and work itself will become a means to an end rather than part of our everyday spiritual life. Marion Derby in her book, *The Zen Environment*, wrote about the general attitude that she felt many Americans have toward work:

> Most people in this country have been conditioned to regard certain kinds of work as respectable and other kinds as menial. This is very unfortunate. It creates a lopsided cultural posture. In Zen monasteries humble tasks, such as weeding the garden or washing the dishes, are considered just as holy as the esoteric ceremonies performed by the priests inside the temple. (78)

In traditional Buddhist societies, on the other hand, work and leisure are often experienced as two sides of the same coin, and the coin itself is understood to be the total expression of spiritual life. Everything from running a board meeting to cleaning the toilet is seen as both useful and meaningful work deserving dignity and appreciation.

In *Small Is Beautiful*, E. F. Schumacher describes Right Livelihood this way:

> The Buddhist point of view takes the function of work to be at least threefold: to give a [person] a chance to utilize and develop

his faculties; to enable him to overcome his ego-centeredness by joining with other people in a common task; and to bring forth the goods and services needed for a becoming existence. (58)

In addition, he writes:

Character, at the same time, is formed primarily by a [person's] work. And work, properly conducted in conditions of human dignity and freedom, blesses those who do it and equally their products. (Ibid.)

I was fortunate enough to follow in my teacher's footsteps, receiving monk ordination and dharma transmission (permission to teach others) from him while continuing to work as an elementary/middle school teacher. Between my serious training with Les and my daily work with children, I was given boundless opportunities to experience Schumacher's view of Buddhist work: developing and utilizing my faculties for teaching others; working with others (both children and adult staff members) in common tasks that required me to drop my self-centered ways in order to maintain harmonious working relationships; and, without necessarily noticing along the way, building my character through years of daily practice in an environment in which others did not necessarily bring the same point of view to their work. My practice, therefore, took place on two fronts: on the one side was daily meditation practice, investigating the fundamental nature of reality by observing my own mind and its habitual tendencies and (hopefully) letting them go moment after moment; on the other side was my active practice in the marketplace where I had to deal with whatever or whomever was in front of me, manifesting the clarity and equanimity arising from my meditation practice in the context of my daily working life.

Even with the example of my teacher's work/practice model, however, I didn't fully realize the importance of Right Livelihood nor experience it in a fully integrated manner until I attended my first extended period of practice at Tassajara Monastery in Northern California. In the early years of my meditation practice, I worked as a freelance graphic designer, the bread and butter work of many starving artists who cannot support themselves solely on the sale of their artwork. As such, I was often expected to create artwork for products or services that felt, if not harmful in obvious ways, at least not particularly helpful in terms of promoting excess consumption and greed. This often left me feeling a bit uncomfortable, but as the work paid the bills, I tended to push my conscience aside, avoiding internal moral arguments that might decrease my marketability.

In 1988, however, I made the decision to do a three-month practice period at Tassajara, putting my graphic design work on hold and leaving the household concerns and the family dog in my husband's care. Those three months turned out to be a life-changing experience in many ways, but especially in terms of how I returned to the workplace. For the first time in my life, I lived communally, sharing both the practice and the daily tasks of life with sixty other individuals for the benefit of all. These daily tasks—work practice, as it was called—took on a whole new meaning for me by being firmly grounded in the Buddhist precepts, as well as the Eightfold Path. Work practice was given the same weight as meditation and was expected to be done with the same level of care and thoughtfulness. Unlike my worldly experience, work wasn't being done for personal gain or benefit, and I was not rewarded in any special way for doing my work with attention—that was just how the work was to be done. Work, I found, was just the *active* side of meditation, a meaningful way of expressing interconnectedness in every activity whether it was cleaning the altar or raking the courtyard—not exactly the way it works in corporate America!

When I returned to my householder life three months later and sat down at my drafting board, I was aghast. I was working alone for the first time in three months, which had never bothered me before my communal experience. In addition, all the tasks that had been shared during my time in the monastery were now mine alone. Something was terribly wrong with this picture! I missed working with others and I missed sharing the joy (and burden) of life's everyday tasks. I felt totally overwhelmed and totally alone.

Within a few short weeks I found myself interviewing at a special progressive school where friends of mine were schooling their children. The school, based on the Quaker values of its founders, aligned beautifully with my own Buddhist values. Teachers and parents worked communally to raise children in a creative and caring atmosphere in which everyone—teachers, parents, and children—benefitted. This was exactly what I experienced at the monastery: everyone working together for the benefit of all beings rather than being concerned only about their individual needs and desires.

Twenty-seven years have passed since I became part of that school where I still teach today, a place where my meditation practice and my daily work are fully integrated. In that time, I also completed training with my Zen teacher, and was given permission to teach others and to start my own sangha. The school became my "marketplace temple" of daily practice where the teachers, children, and parents were my best (and often challenging) teachers. My sangha provided the "practice temple" in which, through meditation and mindfulness activities together, we found ways to support each other in taking our practice back out into the everyday world.

While I am well aware of how unusual it was to find work that aligned so seamlessly with my Buddhist values, and that many others may not be so fortunate, I believe that those values can be brought to any work through an understanding of the practice of Right Livelihood. For many people, work is a pragmatic necessity, a way to put food on the table and provide a home for one's family, in which few options or choices of livelihood may be available due to lack of education or opportunity. For others like myself, there may be opportunities to choose one's livelihood based on preferences and natural talents rather than just necessity. Finally, for a very small minority with independent means, livelihood may be based solely on personal preferences, doing whatever is appealing or personally fulfilling.

As a society, we tend to value work that we choose to do or that has a higher social or economic market value. Right Livelihood, on the other hand, is about valuing all work that is done in a meaningful and useful way and honoring both the work and the one doing the work. In considering the relative value of work, Wendell Berry wrote in *Life is a Miracle*:

> Unlike the culture of the European Middle Ages, which honored the vocations of the learned teacher, the country parson, and the plowman as well as that of the knight, or the culture of Japan in the Edo period which ranked that farmer and the craftsman above the merchant, our own culture places an absolute premium upon various kinds of stardom. This degrades and impoverishes ordinary life, ordinary work, and ordinary experience. It depreciates and underpays work of the primary producers of goods, and of the performers of all kinds of essential but unglamorous jobs and

duties. The inevitable practical results are that most work is now poorly done; great cultural and natural resources are neglected, wasted, or abused; the land and its creatures are destroyed; and the citizenry is poorly taught, poorly governed, and poorly served. (57)

Ordinary life, ordinary work, ordinary experience—for almost every human being, the majority of each person's day is taken up with "ordinary work." Whether that work is in the home raising children, farming the land, teaching, working for a corporation, or providing retail goods or services to the larger community, we all work all day long. Once our "official" job is done for the day, we come home and work there, doing the activities and chores required to take care of ourselves and our families. When we divorce work from honor and dignity by elevating certain forms of work while demeaning others as menial, we diminish the majority of our daily experience to drudgery and despair.

As Berry points out, the practical result of such an attitude means that work becomes merely something to "get done" and, therefore, is not done well, nor is there any real motivation to do so. Inevitably, "the citizenry is poorly taught, poorly governed, and poorly served," not to mention unhappy and unfulfilled, because we are always looking forward to the end of work rather than finding our joy in the work itself. When, on the other hand, we finally understand the truth of our interdependence, we realize that each person's contribution is not only valid but absolutely necessary to the well-being of the whole community. The community needs janitors, cafeteria workers, housecleaners, and ditch-diggers just as surely as it needs inventors, artists, and leaders in government.

Zen teacher, Bernard Glassman, writes:

> The main purpose of our livelihood is to sustain us. We need to make enough money to support ourselves and our family or community. We also need to make enough to put aside some reserves. But in order to truly support and enrich our life, our livelihood has to be more than merely a way to make money . . . . When our livelihood lacks—or contradicts—our spirituality or study or social action, then we won't savor our work. When that's the case, we end up feeling malnourished or burnt out. (*Instructions*, 57)

This is precisely where work and Right Livelihood intersect: work has to be "more than merely a way to make money." Work itself—daily ordinary activity, whatever it is—is our opportunity, moment by moment, to contribute to global harmony and prosperity while at the same time nourishing our own minds and hearts. When work and spirituality are not connected, we will not "savor our work" nor find a way to live a meaningful and useful existence.

The eight limbs of the Eightfold Path are meant to promote and perfect the three essentials of Buddhist training and discipline: wisdom (*prajna*), ethical conduct (*sila*), and mental discipline (*samadhi*). While each of the limbs begins with the word "right," it is important to understand that this is not "right" as opposed to "wrong." Rather, we are meant to understand it as "a spirit of uprightness and truth around studying and asking questions about each of these . . . (Leighton 262)." "Uprightness" includes the pure precepts of doing all good, causing no harm, and benefitting all beings. To truly understand one limb—Right Livelihood, in this case—requires understanding and integrating the other seven. This is why we study the limbs of the path individually as well as together; they are not meant to be rules to be accepted no matter the circumstances, but guidelines that intertwine, affecting and informing each other depending on causes and conditions in this moment.

Of all the limbs of the Eightfold Path, I believe the one that has changed the most since the Buddha's time is Right Livelihood. Right View, for example, is the Buddha's original description of emptiness and karma. It is a transcendent understanding beyond time, space, and culture that has not changed since the Buddha first taught it 2,500 years ago. Similarly Right Intention, as the manifestation of this understanding, and the practices of Right Meditation, Right Mindfulness and Right Effort, which support Right Intention, have not changed significantly since their inclusion as factors in the Eightfold Path. That leaves the three ethical practices of Right Speech, Right Action, and Right Livelihood to consider. While the first two may have changed in terms of content, the essential practice of them relative to our understanding of Right View is fundamentally the same. Right Speech is still based on abstention from lying, slander, or talk that may bring about disharmony. Right Action still aims at promoting moral, honorable, and peaceful conduct in our daily lives. Right Livelihood, however, has changed dramatically since the Buddha's time. While it is essentially about honorable work that is free from harmful consequences, work itself has changed beyond even the Buddha's considerable imagination! From his agrarian-based society, he could not have foreseen the work of modern-day people or the ways in which that work is increasingly at odds with Buddhist values of dignity, kindness, and respect, as well as our fundamental precept of causing no harm.

One of the earliest mentions of Right Livelihood and work practice in Zen literature is a famous story involving the Chinese master, Pai Chang. Dogen relates the story of Pai Chang in the *Shobogenzo* fascicle of *Gyoji* (Ceaseless Practice):

> There was not a single day in the life of Pai-chang . . . from the time he became attendant of Ma-tsu until the evening of his death, when he did not labor to serve people, and to serve his assembly. To our gratitude, he left the words, "A day of no samu [work] is a day of no eating." Pai-chang was at the extreme of old age, and on occasions of "all invited" samu, when everybody labored vigorously, the whole assembly felt pain and regret that their teacher should be included in the work party. At last, at one samu time, some monks hid his tools and would not hand them over. That day, Pai-chang did not eat, as compensation for not using mattock and bamboo basket. He said, "A day of no samu is a day of not eating." (qtd. in Aitken 112-3)

As Dogen observed, these words fill us even today with profound gratitude because they directly address the relationship between work and service, between dignity and usefulness, between caring for others and being cared for by others. In terms of Right Livelihood, these are the values to which Buddhists still adhere and try to practice in daily life. However, the majority of modern-day work in Western society is no longer done with a mattock and bamboo basket; rather, it is more likely to be performed with a computer, phone, or other modern technology. How do we bring our Buddhist values into the current marketplace in which livelihood is based on increasingly abstract occupations that tend to separate us not only from each other, but from the original life-producing sources themselves? As J.C. Kumarappa, an Indian philosopher and economist, once wrote,

> If the nature of the work is properly appreciated and applied, it will stand in the same relation to the higher faculties as food is

to the physical body. It nourishes and enlivens the higher [person] and urges him to produce the best he is capable of. (qtd. in Schumacher 59).

Do our current choices of livelihood fulfill this description of feeling nourished and enlivened in the way that Pai Chang obviously did with his mattock and basket?

In order to consider Right Livelihood in all its complexity, we first need to understand what was originally meant by this limb of the path. In the Buddha's time, Right Livelihood was defined generally as not making a living through harmful acts including killing, deception, or cheating others. Harmful occupations that were specifically prohibited in the Buddha's time included "trading in arms, in living beings, in flesh, in intoxicating drinks, or in poison. Military service and the work of hunter, fisherman, etc., are understood as also included in this list (Sangharakshita, 158)." The underlying meaning of Right Livelihood is to support oneself and one's family by honorable means that are in accord with the precepts. This includes taking into account not only the work itself, which may seem harmless in isolation, but also some knowledge of the consequences of that work and the final product which may actually be quite harmful.

Right Livelihood also includes the idea that people should have some means to support themselves through meaningful activity that allows integrity and dignity, not just for their own benefit, but for all who benefit from their work. This is Schumacher's assertion that "work, properly conducted in conditions of human dignity and freedom, blesses those who do it and equally their products." In the *Anguttara Nikaya*, the Buddha is recorded as saying: "[W]ealth acquired by energetic striving . . . righteously gained . . . makes [one] happy and properly maintains [one] in happiness (Bodhi 126)." The Buddha did not believe that wealth itself was an obstacle to awakening; rather he considered morally just acquisition of wealth or financial security to be a skillful source of happiness. However, wealth was not an end in itself; its value lay in the uses to which it was put including material gifts and gifts of time and attention. In the best of all possible worlds, the work of Right Livelihood would therefore contribute not only to our individual well-being but, through the skillful means of generosity and awareness of the needs of others, to entire communities and global societies, spreading the values of care, kindness, and dignity to the farthest corners of humanity.

This brings us to a core question: what would constitute "Wrong Livelihood"? Clearly it is not wealth per se that gets in our way when it is "obtained through rightful means" and is shared with the world community in a just and meaningful way. Perhaps it is not even the particular work itself that is the issue as our Buddhist precepts can be brought to bear in any situation. The Zen teacher, Lewis Richmond, wrote about Right Livelihood as "[C]onscious livelihood. In other words, regardless of our job (or lack of a job) we should be aware of the implications and consequences of what we do (par. 4)."

If we bring our traditional understanding of Right Livelihood to current occupations around the world, it is fairly obvious that the list of "wrong" livelihoods would include: warring and military careers; hunting, fishing, or butchering; producing and/or selling alcohol, drugs, or other addictive substances; trafficking in human beings including slavery, sexual abuse, and pornography, as well as trafficking in animals for trophies or body parts; and cheating and deception, which could include gamblers, stockbrokers, politicians, or even heads of companies depending on how these individuals pursue their goals and affect others. Have the traditional parameters changed or not?

In his book *Zen Questions*, Zen teacher, Taigen Leighton, examines Right Livelihood as it pertains to war, violence, and the military—areas of endeavor clearly proscribed in the original teachings of the Buddha. In the chapter entitled "Enlightened Patriotism and Right Livelihood," he writes:

> The realities of the modern post-Nazi Holocaust world and post 9/11 world may mean that contemporary Buddhists must acknowledge the necessity for military forces to be used for genuine self-defense, to resist terrorist attacks and hostile occupations, and as peace-keeping forces in situations where genocide or other major harm is being committed. . . . While I deeply wish for complete nuclear disarmament, in the meantime I am very glad that there is a meditation group at the Air Force Academy, and that our Air Force pilots have training in meditative calm. (Leighton 264)

So, while Leighton is a devoted practitioner who holds to the fundamental stricture of Buddhist practice to cause no harm, he also suggests that the realities of our modern world may require a wider interpretation of Right Livelihood based on incredibly complex causes and conditions that didn't exist in the Buddha's time. In this case, Leighton sees the pragmatic need for a military presence for "genuine self-defense . . . and as peace-keeping forces. . . ." However, if a government is going to have a military and train thousands of men and women for such livelihood, the value of a meditation practice for those individuals may mitigate the negative aspect of harmful acts because they "may have the spiritual fortitude to resist if ordered to commit acts contrary to international conventions about war and war crimes (264)."

Are traditionally proscribed livelihoods—warring, trafficking sentient beings, hunting and fishing—now possible to entertain because ultimately they mitigate worse harm? If the occupations of war can become acceptable as Right Livelihood given a particular context, might not the other categories have mitigating circumstances? For instance, the killing of animals has been a part of human civilization since recorded history; ancient caves and pottery from diverse cultures are filled with scenes from the hunt. Native Americans and other tribal cultures world-wide that live close to the land have killed animals of necessity to feed their families. And yet, making your living as a rancher, breeder, or hunter is proscribed on the list of Right Livelihood because it includes killing beings. What about the killing of vegetables and fruits? Are the harvesters of those foods not guilty of killing, too, and therefore not practicing Right Livelihood? Robert Aitken Roshi is purported to have once said, "The only difference between a cow and a vegetable is that the cow screams louder." The fact remains that everything we eat has died before coming to our table; it is merely our human judgment that distinguishes the relative value of a chicken versus a bean plant. Both must give their lives so that we may live.

Perhaps "wrong livelihood" has more to do in this case with the manner in which the killing is done and for what final purpose. Killing an animal purely for purposes of sport or for body parts for exotic aphrodisiacs is in quite a different category than for the purpose of providing food for one's family. Honoring the death of another being so that we may live and killing in a safe and humane way also changes the nature of the death itself by arousing our gratitude and appreciation for the life given.

Prostitution—the trafficking of human bodies for sexual purposes—is an equally complicated question. Egregious poverty in combination with lack of education means that many young women and men have little alternative to starvation than to use the one thing they have to offer—their bodies. While the individuals who profit from their bodies and those who seek out such services are clearly practicing or contributing to the practice of wrong livelihood, are the prostitutes themselves? Again, might it be possible for someone to prostitute her body—something clearly proscribed by the path of Right Livelihood—if it is her only means of supporting her family?

Finally, what about cheating and deception? In the Buddha's time, I'm sure there were professional gamblers running games of chance, as well as moneylenders charging exorbitant rates of interest. Both professions were probably guilty of cheating and deception and therefore came under the Buddha's proscription in terms of Right Livelihood. Both occupations still exist today, but the cheating and deception that currently takes place around money staggers the imagination because of two main differences.

First, in the Buddha's time, actual coins or goods were exchanged, making deception harder to accomplish; today most transactions are electronic, and without the checks and balances of seeing or touching what is being exchanged, deception and cheating become not only more tempting, but more possible.

Second, with the exception of making interest on borrowed money, there was no idea in the Buddha's time of using someone else's money to make more money. Take, for example, the stock market where this practice is not only allowed by law, but is a respectable occupation worldwide. While there are probably many honest workers in this profession, it is an occupation rife with temptations: one can profit by the ignorance or greed of clients, using their money with which to gamble rather than one's own. This means there is very little motivation to be honest or cautious—after all, if the money gets lost and the fund dries up, the individual stockbroker can always blame the banking system for the loss, never needing to accept the responsibility or consequences of his own recklessness or dishonesty. So, while the profession of stockbroker may in and of itself fall into the category of Right Livelihood in which "wealth acquired by energetic striving . . . righteously gained . . . makes [one] happy and properly maintains [one] in happiness" as the Buddha said, it may also be a tremendously harmful occupation that ruins the lives of innocent people who put their trust in that individual.

For Buddhist practitioners Right Livelihood clearly needs to align with the ethical guidelines of the precepts and the Eightfold Path, including the overall admonition to cause no harm. However, as we have already seen, some livelihoods that may have been proscribed in the past may now be acceptable in certain conditions. However, without falling into the delusion of rationalization, how are we to discern what truly constitutes Right Livelihood in the twenty-first century?

Perhaps it is less about the work we do, but how we do it and what intentions we bring to it. Randy Komisar, a partner in a venture capital firm in Silicon Valley, as well as a long-term practitioner of the dharma, expresses it this way:

> Today we are confronted with more ambiguity about right and wrong than people faced two thousand years ago. The interdependencies of all things and the global consequences of our actions are more evident every day in media and public discourse. The truth appears flexible. Right and wrong results depend on one's perspective. The Buddha foresaw some of this in pronouncing the interdependency of all things. And he gave us a compass—our good intentions. By being thoughtful of others, seeing that there are no others, and acting with right intent we have a path toward right livelihood. Imperfect as we all are, this path may have consequences we prefer to disavow, but we must proceed with compassion and understanding. (Personal interview)

It is crucial to remember that Right Livelihood does not exist in a vacuum, but must always be considered in the context of its relationship to the other seven limbs of the Eightfold Path. As part of the triad of *sila* (ethical conduct), Right Livelihood clearly includes both Right Speech and Right Action, but it is equally important to observe it through the lens of Right View. In a world that is increasingly abstract, technical, and lacking in human interaction and oversight, ethical decisions become increasingly abstract as well, often leading to a rationalizing mindset in which ends justify means. As Komisar observes, when this happens, "the truth appears flexible." Our ideas of right and wrong begin to depend more on our individual and personal perspective, which is often clouded by the three poisons of desire, aversion, and delusion, rather than on the universal view of benefitting all beings.

Without taking into account Right Speech and Right Action, or understanding our interdependence expressed in Right View, work that includes aspects antithetical to beneficial action (or which actually cause harm) might seem acceptable if the ends are proved to be beneficial in some measurable way. Outsourcing work to other countries, for instance, may provide cheap goods and services for the American consumer—a perceived benefit to us—but often comes at the price of those individuals being poorly paid and working in sub-standard conditions without benefits, not to mention the possible loss of jobs here in our own country.

From the viewpoint of Right Livelihood, perhaps it is helpful to ask ourselves why we work and what is its purpose in our lives? Is it strictly for our own self-aggrandizement and promotion, or is work itself—the dignity and satisfaction of a challenge met or a job well done that benefits both self and other—the purpose of work? Ezra Bayda writes:

> Perhaps the one question that we don't ask often enough is, "What do I have to offer?" We are so intent on analyzing what we can get from a job or an occupation that we rarely consider the sense of satisfaction that comes from offering our unique contribution. (*Being Zen*, 96)

In other words, perhaps part of Right Livelihood is reflecting upon our choice of work by asking "what can I *give*" rather than "what do I *get*." As interdependent beings, perhaps Right Livelihood is the way that we can intentionally provide for ourselves and our families, while at the same time contributing to universal well-being and harmony.

As Komisar observes, the Buddha "gave us a compass—our good intentions." However, in order to read this compass and reckon our direction on the path of Right Livelihood, we need to understand what is meant by intention. Intention has three aspects: discernment, commitment, and perseverance. Discernment—the insight, awareness, and clarity that arises in our mind in meditation—allows us to form beneficial intentions that align with our understanding of the wisdom and compassion contained in the Eightfold Path and the Buddhist precepts. Once we have formed these intentions, we need to make a commitment to uphold them, continually questioning whether our work is being performed in view of them. Finally, intentions require perseverance; we cannot throw them aside at the first obstacle, nor try to find an easier path by rationalizing the need for the parts that are not aligning with our spiritual practice.

As Buddhist practitioners, our deepest intention is to benefit all beings while causing no harm. When we diligently apply this intention to our daily work in combination with our practice of the Eightfold Path and the Buddhist precepts, our work *becomes* spiritual practice and Right Livelihood very naturally appears.

Works cited

Aitken, Robert. *The Mind of Clover*. New York: North Point, 1984.

Bayda, Ezra. *Being Zen*. Boston: Shambala, 2003.

Berry, Wendell. *Life is a Miracle*. Berkeley, CA: Counterpoint, 2001.

Bodhi, Bhikkhu, ed. *In the Buddha's Words: An Anthology of Discourses from the Pali Canon*. Boston: Wisdom, 2005.

Glassman, Bernard. *Instructions to the Cook*. New York: Bell Tower, 1996.

Komisar, Randy. *Personal interview*. Sept. 2015.

Leighton, Taigen Dan. " Enlightened Patriotism and Right Livelihood." *Zen Questions: Zazen, Dogen, and the Spirit of Creative Inquiry*. Somerville, MA: Wisdom, 2011.

Mountain, Marion Derby. *The Zen Environment*. New York: William Morrow, 1982.

Richmond, Lewis. "Buddhism and Wealth: Defining Right Livelihood." *Huffington Post: Religion* 16 March 2011. <http://www.huffingtonpost.com/lewis-richmond/right-livelihood-is-consc_b_832298.html>. Excerpt from *Work as a Spiritual Practice*. Potter/TenSpeed/Harmony, 1999.

Sangharakshita. *A Survey of Buddhism*. London: Tharpa, 1987.

Schumacher, E. F. *Small is Beautiful*. New York: Harper, 1989.

CHAPTER 6

Right Effort: Learning To Fly

Teijo Munnich

Over the past year I have put much of my concentration on Right Effort, partly to collect my thoughts to write this chapter, but mostly because this is the part of the Eightfold Path that I have found most challenging to understand. Since I first encountered Right Effort some forty years ago, I have wanted to understand it and how it works in human life, so I've been thinking about this for a while and I've gained some insights.

This is partially due to my study of the teachings of Dogen Zenji. I've become more aware of a thread of non-discrimination in Dogen's writing—or should I say Dogen has helped me see the subtle way that we humans discriminate. Again and again in his teachings Dogen advises us to recognize the oneness of Life, how everything is interconnected even beyond what we can understand. Because of this influence, I became interested in looking at Right Effort from the perspective of non-discrimination.

I began writing this just after the deaths of two good friends and just before the death of my Aunt Claire, with whom I spent the last week of her life. We expected her death a year earlier, but she rallied for another twelve months with the support of hospice, still not missing a church dinner, family Christmas party, or birthday. She died shortly after her ninety-seventh birthday. I went to stay with her for two weeks the first time we thought she was dying. At that time she indicated that she didn't think it was necessary for me to be there, so when she asked for me the following year as she once again faced death, I was surprised. I thought that she wanted to die alone as she was a very independent woman. When I heard she had asked for me, I quickly made a plane reservation for the following morning and flew to Minneapolis from North Carolina to spend her last days with her. The deaths of my two friends and being with my aunt during her last week of life brought death front and center in my consciousness. As I confront the reality of death and grief as much as I ever have in my life, I ask myself, "What is Right Effort now?"

So, mingled with my thoughts about effort, and Dogen Zenji's teachings about non-discrimination, I've had to acknowledge that Right Effort for me right now is writing this chapter in the midst of a process that I identify as "grief." I found while I was reflecting on effort that something was nagging at me, something that prevented me from speaking about it in more than a superficial way. I tried to put the feelings aside so I could concentrate on what I wanted to say, but I couldn't do that until I looked at Right Effort in relation to grief.

What is grief and how does it relate to Right Effort? I can say what has happened to me when I've encountered death closely in the past. After the sudden death of my sister, I often could not hold a thought long enough to act on it or to write it down. At other times when someone close to me died, I found myself thinking of everything I did in relation to my own death; for example, if I should suddenly die, how would the things I do be taken care of? I've experienced the closeness of death, that I could die at any time. And when someone close to me dies, I've felt that part of me dies. This is all, I think, part of the grieving process.

In trying to help Aunt Claire face her death, I experienced the very real question of what is next after human life? It's not something I really want to think about, but it has become very present in my mind and I cannot ignore it. I also know this is an opportunity to face fear of death—but how? My teacher, Katagiri Roshi, told us a story about when Shunryu Suzuki Roshi was dying and some of his students asked him for some Zen wisdom; his response was "I don't want to die."

A family member of my friend Jan, who died just before my aunt died, called me when Jan was in hospice and told me that Jan wanted to talk with me. Jan was on speaker phone and, among other things, she said, "Teijo, I'm afraid to die." I was completely unable to say anything. When one is facing death, that is surely when the real fear comes up, and I knew she was facing something I've never faced, so I really know nothing about it. I had the impulse to offer incense, so I did, telling her what I was doing as I did it. As I offered the incense, it occurred to me to chant. I asked her if that was okay and she said she would like that. I sat down at the bells and started chanting everything I knew in English and Japanese. I don't know how long I chanted, but when I stopped it was very quiet on the other end of the line. Then her husband came back on the phone. She was sleeping restfully after a few very agitated days. The next day I received an update from her daughter. "Mom says it is starting to make sense, how to die. She is scared, but understands that it is scary because it is new, and things that are new get less scary the more we do them." This is Right Effort.

I'm skeptical when people tell me they're not afraid of death. Any transition in life requires stepping into the unknown and adjusting our perspective. Death is the ultimate transition and really, the ultimate unknown. Aunt Claire was devoutly religious, and that was a great advantage to her as she lay dying. People came to her bedside and prayed with her; choir members came and sang for her; communion was brought to her until she could no longer swallow; and she was bathed in love and caring by friends and family. Still, I sensed fear, as if she were facing a blank wall and didn't really know what was on the other side. Whatever she believed, it seemed that she still had some question, and she was afraid to die.

Transitions in life are difficult. Even moving into what we know to be a better situation is often difficult because we never really know for sure what it will be like. At least our current situation is familiar, and yet, because of impermanence we can't really hold on to anything. In every moment everything in life is changing, though that change may be imperceptible. This is reality. We can see it in flowers and vegetables, in animals, in all forms of life. Science tells us that we replace every cell in our body every seven years. This is impermanence. Even though we know this intellectually and can see it in the world around us, facing our own impermanence is problematic. We really do die in every moment, but our minds try to hold on to what we already know.

In the *Shukke-kudoku* (The Merit of Leaving Family Life) fascicle of his *Shobogenzo*, Dogen Zenji says: "There are six billion, four hundred million, ninety-nine thousand, nine hundred eighty moments in a day and night, and the five skandhas [we humans] are born and perish at each moment, but we don't notice it (Tanahashi 803)." If you try to break this statement down to understand what it means (i.e., how many moments in an hour, how many moments in a minute . . .), it boggles the mind. If Dogen is correct, then there are about two-hundred-fifty million moments in an hour and about four million moments in a minute, both numbers a little hard to wrap one's head around. Dogen's point is that

113

our minds cannot possibly keep up with such fast-changing reality, yet we are part of that constant movement.

I think that Right Effort is very connected with death—our fear of it and our willingness to face it squarely when the opportunity arises. And we have many opportunities. When we feel we have failed, this is the death of our perception of how things should be. A breakup or a loss is a death—of something or someone that has meaning for us, that gives us a feeling of connection. When we encounter death of any kind, we have the choice to ignore it or to take a step towards it, to face it directly. Ignoring something doesn't change its reality; it just drives fear deeper.

In *When Things Fall Apart*, Pema Chodron tells a story about a ferocious dog that broke loose and ran towards her teacher Trungpa Rinpoche and his attendants: "The attendants screamed and froze in terror. Rinpoche turned and ran as fast as he could—straight at the dog. The dog was so surprised that he put his tail between his legs and ran away (14-15)." I suspect that even Rinpoche felt some fear as he ran towards the dog, but he went forward recognizing that he was afraid of the source of fear, which is simply the unknown. By being aware that we're afraid but running toward that fear anyway, the fear can become known and no longer has such a hold on us.

Looking Into The Words, Opening To Meaning

If facing our fears is the essence of Right Effort, how do we practice that? I think we can get a broader understanding of the practice of Right Effort by looking at different translations of the Pali words *samma* (Right) and *vayama* (Effort). Using very specific English words can be misleading, particularly when the original meanings are multidimensional. In *Each Moment is the Universe*, Katagiri Roshi said:

> The word "right" isn't based on an idea of right and wrong, good and bad. Right means the complete, perfect harmony of the phenomenal world of time, which we create from moment to moment, and the source of existence, the eternal world of timelessness, where all sentient beings are always interconnected in peace and harmony. (125-6)

Samma or "right" means "to go along with, to go together, to turn together" literally "to unite [with]." We usually think of "right" as something in opposition to what we identify as "wrong." This implies there is a kind of effort that is acceptable and desirable and another kind of effort that is unacceptable and undesirable. Of course it cannot be denied that the source and quality of our effort affects the result, but making these distinctions is somewhat artificial because they are based on speculation or past experience.

Vayama or "effort" has a broader meaning than can be expressed with any single English word. In addition to "effort," it has been translated as diligence, enthusiasm, and zeal. Dogen Zenji emphasizes diligence in his *Shobogenzo* fascicle *Hachidainingaku* (Eight Awakenings of Great Beings):

> The Buddha said, "Monks, if you make diligent effort, nothing is too difficult. That's why you should do so. It is like a thread of water piercing through a rock by constantly dripping. If your mind continues to slacken, it is like taking a break from hitting stones before they spark; you can't get fire that way. What I am speaking of is 'diligent effort.' " (Okumura, trans. 3)

The Buddha doesn't say what we should do, he simply points to the value of putting one foot in front of the other. Whatever we do, if we stick with it, we will learn something about what we are doing through the process of doing it. But it isn't a slam dunk. Anything we want to do or learn from takes time and patience. When trying to start Great Tree Zen Women's Temple, I often felt that all I really needed to do was to take care of my own practice and things would fall into place. This meant I had to remember that the most important reason for Great Tree was the practice, not the physical space or any version of the vision that I or anyone else had. Though it was hard for me when I felt failure, learning to return to the practice has helped me let go of how I think things should be and appreciate what is.

Enthusiasm or zeal supports diligence. Even in those moments when we feel our efforts are not successful, we can continue by keeping our deep intention alive in our awareness. Results may not be what we expected yet we continue because we understand the importance of our vision or our intention. When we first started Great Tree, it was because of a vision I had of exploring another perspective of a practice that I felt was not being adequately considered—bringing more balance, perhaps, to the Zen world as I had experienced it. From the beginning of my Zen practice—in Minnesota, California, and Japan—I found myself in a male-dominated world, and one day I realized that, although I loved the practice, I felt my insights weren't being heard or understood. It's hard to articulate just how powerfully that awareness hit me, this sudden notion to create a practice place where women could support each other and strengthen each other's insights by hearing them and understanding them. Being heard and understood is something I experienced in all-girls Catholic schools, and what at times I felt was missing in my Zen practice. What might be called enthusiasm or zeal for this goal carried me through some very difficult times in the development of Great Tree, even those times when I really wanted to quit. It manifested as sticking with it until I had no other options, choosing to continue to take one step after another until I had left no stone unturned. Sometimes I wanted to quit, but deep down I knew that if I didn't continue to try until there was no more that could be done, I would regret giving up too soon. No sense of right or wrong, just stepping into the unknown with a clear intention.

ALL EFFORT IS RIGHT EFFORT

> Right means the complete, perfect harmony of the phenomenal world of time, which we create from moment to moment, and the source of existence, the eternal world of timelessness, where all sentient beings are always interconnected in peace and harmony. (Katagiri 125-6)

In an absolute sense, all effort is Right Effort because the origin of Right Effort is present in every one of us whether we recognize it or not. Right Effort, in the context of the "eternal world of timelessness," is effort that supports the "complete, perfect harmony" and balance all forms of life innately seek. If we act in ways that create disharmony, it takes more energy to restore the balance. With awareness, we can learn to act in ways that are in harmony with how things are in each moment. If we don't understand that life moves toward harmony and balance, we might act in ways that create disharmony.

To say that all effort is Right Effort might raise the argument that if effort is directed towards something that causes disharmony, it cannot be called "right"; yet to make distinctions such as "good effort" and "bad effort" can itself be the source of disharmony. When we judge situations based on a concrete definition of what is good and what is bad, we apply habitual responses to situations we judge to be similar to those we have faced in the past without making an effort to be aware of what is actually happening in each moment. Just as taking the same medicine for every illness could create serious imbalances—or just not work—Right Effort involves being in sync with the circumstances of each moment and then allowing action to emerge from that reality.

While the origin of Right Effort is present in every one of us, if we don't engage directly with life, we might act in ways that create disharmony. To experience freedom through effort, we must step into each moment fearlessly and respond to what is needed in that moment. Sometimes this means charging forward; sometimes it requires holding back; sometimes it means to simply put one foot in front of the other.

One might argue that acting with the intention to create disharmony might be seen as "wrong" effort. I would argue that, rather than intending disharmony, we humans inadvertently bring it about by our self-centeredness, by exclusively focusing on what "I" need, what "I" want, what will make "me" feel good. When we think only of our own wishes, we are inclined to do whatever is necessary to make something happen without considering how it affects everything around us. When we cannot see our effort holistically, our effort does not synchronize with life, and this creates disharmony. I believe that all people are searching for the experience of oneness, which we typically seek in relationships, both social and personal. I think we're all trying to experience a connection with Life that is already present. This, I believe, is the origin of effort whether "right" or "wrong."

When I talk about "Life," I mean the many forms of life interacting with and supporting each other. I don't believe there is a force called "evil" that exists as an entity that is separate from "good." I believe that everything arises because of everything else, that everything is always seeking balance, and that what we might interpret as an opposing force is arising to bring balance to the situation.

So I really don't think "evil" is ever intended, but rather effort that may have disharmonious results comes about when it arises from an impulse to take care of the self to the exclusion of others. When we do things solely for personal satisfaction, disharmony can easily be the result, because our effort is centered on "me" instead of on our interdependent relationship with all beings.

The value of understanding that the deep intention of all effort is to experience unity is that we cease judging people as good or bad because of their actions or what we perceive as their intentions. This is valuable for us because judgment creates fear and when we are free from fear, we are free. It is valuable for others because when we understand their deep wish for unity, our understanding may help to free them from their misperceptions about how to find it.

> [A]ccording to Dogen it is not because of our individual effort that the moon reflects itself on the water. What Dogen is pointing out here is the reality of all beings as interdependent origination. Everything is connected with everything. Everything exists only within the relationship it has with all other things and by support from them. (Okumura, *Dharma Eye* 9)

What we call "Life" might be described as myriad beings moving together and supporting each other in ways we can name and ways we do not understand. So Life is many beings living interdependently. And everything is changing constantly. This constant change means that all forms of life are constantly responding and adjusting to find balance because the movement of Life is constantly reconfiguring all beings.

How does this relate to Right Effort? The effort we make is movement. Even our thoughts are movement—thoughts, feelings, perceptions, impulses, consciousness—all are movement. Most movement in Life is imperceptible to us, yet every movement affects the whole. Within that context, Right Effort means to be aware of what is happening when it's happening so that our movement is appropriate to the situation. When we are not aware and we apply too much effort or too little effort, other beings are affected and begin looking for the balance. When we are aware, even if we notice gaps in our awareness that bring up compulsiveness or resistance, the very noticing of these gaps is Right Effort, and the balancing begins right there, beyond our effort. This is all Right Effort.

GETTING YOURSELF TO THE CUSHION IS RIGHT EFFORT

My first thought when I encountered Right Effort as a young practitioner was that Right Effort is just getting yourself to the meditation cushion. Some forty years later, this is also my final conclusion. The awareness that is cultivated by just sitting down and shutting up brings freedom to our lives even beyond what we can see. I once heard Katagiri Roshi say something to the effect of: "We live by our effort, but not only by our effort—we are also supported by all beings."

For me Right Effort is to take that step into the unknown, not for the purpose of stepping out of life, but to step *into* life. We prefer to have challenges that we can meet, which are not really challenges at all. We want to feel confident about what we do, so we stay within the realm of knowing.

Buddhist practice challenges us to not know because everything is always changing, so there is nothing that we can know for certain. We are always stepping into the unknown, whether we are aware of it or not. We tell ourselves that we understand. We create stories to convince ourselves that there is something to know. Then, if we don't understand, we believe that somewhere someone exists who does understand, that there must be an explanation. Sitting quietly in meditation (zazen) gives us a place to notice and become aware, to rest in the unknown. Right Effort emerges directly from awareness and is also the source of awareness. When we "just sit" on the meditation cushion (*shikantaza*) we both experience full awareness of what is happening in the moment, and the "effort" of getting ourselves to the cushion and sitting quietly becomes the source of renewed effort

So I return to the fact that processing the deaths of close family and friends has left me with a better idea of what Right Effort is. It is being aware of, and walking towards, the unity that *samma* implies. It is about non-discrimination. While trying to support my aunt in her dying process, I tried to understand what she needed. As she was a devout Catholic, I found myself telling her that death was to unite with God. I do not have a definition of what God is except to say that my perception is that Life itself is what we actually merge with, and within Life we find unity.

It is difficult to put a deadline on grieving. Trying to write this chapter I found that I could not simply put my grief aside in order to write. Some say that when someone dies, you should just get over it and move on. I believe that grieving is a process and also an opportunity to see life as it really is. Anytime we experience loss of any kind, we have this opportunity. And how is life really? It's changing, constantly, every nanosecond. If the message we are giving ourselves is that something is wrong, or we need to just deal with it, we are deluding ourselves. There is nothing we can do to "get over" loss, it's a process that we have to allow without any expectations.

> Right Effort is not something we do, but something we allow to emerge as we step into the unknown, facing our fear while with each step we confirm the harmony and unity of Life. (Millin, personal email)

As I dealt with various kinds of death over the past year, my effort focused on accepting the emotional response, letting go, and stepping into the unknown. My grieving process took hold of me, and I found it hard to ignore while I was trying to understand Right Effort. When something is so personal, one can feel as if others don't want to hear about it; but when I allowed the reality of my experience to have its voice and responded to what was actually happening for me, I felt as if I were coming out of a fog and clarity began to emerge. When we step into the unknown, we are able to experience directly what is happening in our lives. It's also uncomfortable and can be scary, and it seems easier to put it on the back burner and distance ourselves from it. It's counter-intuitive to embrace our discomfort, yet when we allow Right Effort to emerge and experience life as it really is, the fear begins to dissipate and Life embraces us back and supports us. Katagiri Roshi used to always tell us that the purpose of this practice is to learn to live in peace and harmony with all beings. That wish for unity is the source of all effort.

About a month ago I popped an Al Green CD into my car player and since then the song "How can you mend a broken heart?" has been running through my head. I've tried to put it aside, as it makes me very emotional, and I felt I needed clarity to get this chapter written. This morning as the song played in my mind during zazen, I realized that this—heartbreak—is the theme of my life right now. When I noticed this, I thought, "So what is Right Effort in light of that?" Usually we associate heartbreak with the end of a relationship or with feeling romantically rejected, not as something that results from the death of an aunt or from being allowed to participate in the death of a friend. This is why we have difficulty knowing how to practice Right Effort. We have to awaken first to what is actually happening before we can know how to respond.

Life just isn't that clear. We are always walking into the unknown.

Learning To Fly: A Parable

From 1986 to 1988 I lived at Hosshinji Monastery in Obama Japan. During that time I had three dreams about flying. In the first dream, a little girl asked me to take her flying. Though I'd never flown before, I really loved this child, so I was very motivated to try. I put her on my back, flapped my arms very hard, and was able to lift off the ground about three feet. When I woke, I felt pretty good about just getting off the ground.

In my second dream, the same little girl asked me again to take her flying. This time she wanted to go higher, so I tried much harder, flapping my arms with greater intensity. But the result was pretty much the same—we got about four feet off the ground. I noted that this wasn't really flying, and I wondered why such intense effort produced such unsatisfactory results.

About a year later I had the third dream. Putting the little girl on my back, I lifted off the ground and we flew through the sky effortlessly. When I woke up, I felt a freedom I'd never felt before. Something inside me had shifted, though I couldn't put my finger on what or when it was.

When I first began practicing at Hosshinji monastery, I noticed a lot of resistance. Although I imagined that simply following a schedule would be a freeing experience, I was so used to having time when I could do as I wished that I felt this lifestyle to be very restricting. Additionally, there were things I just didn't enjoy doing. My only options were to follow the schedule or to leave. I was motivated to be there, but my effort didn't get me very far off the ground.

As time passed, things became easier in the monastery. I threw myself into the practice and the resistance subsided a bit. Still, my effort was greater than any results I was seeing, and resistance was still present. I was still only four feet off the ground.

Somewhere along the line, I fell into the rhythm of the monastery. I didn't notice it as it was happening, but one of my friends pointed it out to me one day. One of my biggest resistances had been *takuhatsu*, mendicant begging, and she noticed that I seemed to be enjoying it. "Yes," I said, "I do like it. It's a very powerful practice." I was surprised and happy to recognize that there had been a shift; I had come to appreciate the value of *takuhatsu* and many other practices I didn't like. And I came to realize that these practices weren't valuable only for me—my life affected everyone around me.

For example, in *takuhatsu* practice we walked through the streets in a line and chanted, sharing the *dharma* (teachings). In return, people came out of their homes and work places and gratefully offered money, food, whatever they could. It was their way of participating and supporting something they also believed in. I experienced their joy and devotion when they made their offerings, and it touched my heart. Many aspects of Zen practice became apparent to me in this way. One day, as I was walking through the streets in the *takuhatsu* line, I felt a wonderful opening in my heart, and I realized that I was facing in the direction I was going, that I was doing what was truly in my heart—no longer looking back, no longer resisting. I was truly flying.

Works cited

Chodron, Pema. *When Things Fall Apart: Heart Advice For Difficult Times.* Boston: Shambhala, 1999.

Dogen, Eihei. "Shukke-kodoku (The Merit of Leaving Family Life)." *Treasury of the True Dharma Eye: Zen Master Dogen's Shobo Genzo.* Ed. and trans. Kazuaki Tanahashi. 2 vols. Boston: Shambhala, 2010.

Katagiri, Dainin. *Each Moment Is The Universe: Zen and the Way of Being Time.* Boston: Shambhala, 2008.

Okumura, Shohaku. "Dogen Translation." *Dharma Eye.* October 2001: 23.

Okumura, Shohaku, trans. "Hachidainingaku (Eight Awakenings of Great Beings)." Unpublished.

Millin, Peggy. Email to the author. 28 Mar. 2016.

CHAPTER 7

Right Mindfulness: Remembering Reality

Hoko Karnegis

One can hardly pick up a magazine or read a blog today without encountering somebody's views on mindfulness. It's become the darling of self-help programs, corporate coaches and therapists. Advocates hasten to assure us that while mindfulness has roots in Buddhism, these can be ignored in the interest of making it available to the widest possible audience. One need not maintain any connection to the religious tradition from which mindfulness comes, they say, in order to experience its benefits: remaining calm under stress, improved relationships, and healing the wounds of the past.

However, all this is not what Buddhist mindfulness has traditionally been about. Mindfulness has undergone a long and winding journey since the time of Shakyamuni, when it was aimed at freeing one from the grip of craving and aversion, to the time of Dogen, when it became a means of experiencing the one reality, to the modern West, where it's become a popular self-help technique. How did we get here? What do we lose when we take mindfulness out of context? What is the role of mindfulness in Soto Zen and how can we effectively practice with it in our daily lives?

THE FOUR FOUNDATIONS

The Four Foundations of Mindfulness found in the *Satipatthana Sutra* are familiar to Buddhist practitioners around the world. Dogen Zenji reminded his monks of this teaching in a dharma hall discourse:

> Our Buddha [Sakyamuni] said to his disciples, "There are four foundations of mindfulness on which people should depend. These four foundations of mindfulness refer to contemplating the body as impure; contemplating sensation as suffering; contemplating mind as impermanent; and contemplating phenomena as non-substantial."

These teachings were designed to disenchant early Buddhist practitioners with the phenomenal world and help them loosen the grip of craving and aversion. However, Dogen went on to explain that he perceived the four foundations in a whole new way:

> I, Eihei, also have four foundations of mindfulness: contemplating the body as a skin-bag; contemplating sensation as eating bowls; contemplating mind as fences, walls, tiles and pebbles; and contemplating phenomena as old man Zhang drinking wine, old man Li getting drunk. (Leighton and Okumura 287)

Dogen's particular view of mindfulness is based on nonduality of subject and object. In other words, there is nothing of which one is mindful, and no one maintaining something called "mindfulness." While he doesn't take issue with the Buddha regarding the early teachings about mindfulness, Dogen goes beyond the usual conclusions about these elements to see the phenomenal world simply as it is. While his teaching, like that of the Buddha, aims to help us loosen the grip of craving and aversion, it is designed not to discourage engagement with the world, but to allow for full immersion in the world and for the understanding that all things are interconnected. Thus Dogen's foundations for mindfulness are very much about experience of the world and maintaining awareness of nonseparation right in the midst of daily encounters, keeping everything in context. They are about remembering reality.

THE EVOLUTION OF MINDFULNESS

How did this shift in the meaning of mindfulness happen? The earliest Buddhist teachings say that all things that arise in the phenomenal world are products of the twelvefold chain of dependent origination (ignorance, fabrications, consciousness, name and form, six sense bases, contact, feeling, craving, clinging, becoming, birth). Rather than seeing the world as a kind of wondrous web of life and identifying with it, early Buddhists saw it as a mass of suffering. They saw that things arise because we are ignorant and attached, and that these things are ultimately unsatisfying. Thus, they wanted to do what the Buddha did: reverse the chain of causation in order to eliminate ignorance, the root of suffering. In other words, they wanted to dissociate from or disidentify with the phenomenal world that results from the contact of senses with sense-objects.

Today, we may think of the chain of dependent origination or causation as a kind of scientific explanation for how natural phenomena are created. That's completely different from the view of the early Buddhists, who used it to show how life within the cycle of death and rebirth is unsatisfactory. For them, contemplating the chain of causation encouraged disenchantment with the phenomenal world and with one's delusive desires for impermanent things. Such contemplation was an encouragement toward the liberation that results from destroying ignorance, the root of the entire chain. Mindfulness of the impurity of the body, the suffering brought about by the senses, the impermanence of what happens in the mind, and the insubstantiality of the things to which we cling allowed early Buddhists to let go of their attachments to the phenomenal world of birth and death and move toward the liberation of nirvana.

Early Buddhists engaged in four kinds of mindfulness practice: simple, protective, introspective, and deliberate conceptions. Simple mindfulness is non-judgmental observation and recognition of whatever arises. The practitioner does not draw any conclusions or write any stories about what's happening but, recalling earlier experiences, may recognize various elements. Protective mindfulness involves preventing unwholesome states, such as greed or dissatisfaction, from arising by cultivating awareness of one's mental reactions to data received about the objects of the senses. Introspective mindfulness steps in when protective mindfulness has failed to restrain the senses and unwholesomeness has arisen. Practitioners remind themselves to examine their mental states, to recognize whether or not they are wholesome, and to discard those that are detrimental. Finally, in the deliberate forming of conceptions, the practitioner calls to mind what is wholesome and beneficial to serve as inspiration and what is unpleasant to counteract craving. For example, cultivating loving-kindness toward all beings may involve imagining them as one's children; imagining the body as a decaying corpse is a means of loosening attachment to it.

Early Buddhists employed mindfulness to monitor sensory perceptions, to correctly identify what was real, to determine what was to be abandoned, to notice when attention was wandering, and to keep things on an even keel. From their perspective, mindfulness was a support for the analysis that made possible the arising of wisdom and of liberation from the phenomenal world and the wheel of birth and death.

The rise of Mahayana Buddhism at the beginning of the Common Era shifted the focus of Buddhist practice and introduced the bodhisattva ideal. Rather than transcending the phenomenal world, the practitioner's goal became to live an awakened life in the world by seeing through delusion to how things really are. According to the Mahayana tradition, seeing the chain of dependent origination, or seeing the emptiness of all things, is itself awakening, because the world is a manifestation of cosmic reality. It's the difference between seeing the emptiness of the phenomenal world and using dissociation from it to wake up versus awakening by seeing emptiness and becoming one with the source of that phenomenal world—universal reality itself. The teachings evolve from an emphasis on no-self to a teaching that we are in reality a great cosmic self, and the Buddha becomes a transcendent being with whom we're already identical.

When Buddhism came to China in the first century CE, it encountered a culture very different from that of India. Ascetic practice, a renunciation of life in the world, was relatively common in India; Chinese culture emphasized living in the world while understanding that one was a part of it rather than trying to transcend it. If the things of the world, particularly the natural world, have Buddha-nature, as the Mahayana view teaches, then Chinese people wanted to live in the midst of that interdependent web to gain insight into their own Buddha-nature. The world itself was a place of awakening, and seeing interdependence right in this daily world was awakening itself. In this context, mindfulness is less about focusing on any one element in order to realize its unsatisfactoriness and more about cultivating a naturally-arising awareness of the interdynamic functioning of the systems of the universe.

THE PROBLEM OF WORDS

To understand what mindfulness meant to Dogen, it helps to look at the pedigree of the word to see what it actually represents. The original Sanskrit word is *smrti* (Pali: *sati*), "that which is remembered." We've seen already that early mindfulness practices often involved recognizing various elements, remembering to examine mental states, or calling to mind motivational images. When Buddhism reached China, *smrti* was translated as *nian* 念 with a character that contains two components, *jin* ("now") and *xin* ("heart-mind"). In Japanese, the same character, sometimes pronounced *nen*, can mean "attention," "feeling," "desire," or "idea." The original Sanskrit element of memory has not been lost, however, because nen also means "calling to mind" or "remembrance," sometimes particularly relating to carrying forward a sacred tradition and the guidelines taught by generations of teachers.

This "mind of now" became "mindfulness" when it reached the West. The word had existed in English since the 1500s with the meaning of "paying attention to" or "regarding" something. In the late 1800s, Pali language scholar Thomas William Rhys Davids translated *sati* as "mindfulness" in the sense of "a constant presence of mind."

Indeed, in common English usage, "mindfulness" is usually about paying attention. To mind your mother is to take heed of her instructions. To mind your manners is to be careful of your behavior. To mind children is to watch them and keep them out of trouble. "Don't mind me," we say when we walk in on people engaged in an important conversation, encouraging them not to pay any attention to us while we grab that forgotten item and slip out the door.

It may seem then that Right Mindfulness is about directing our attention to what's in front of us, really concentrating on it, and not being distracted by whatever else is happening inside and outside of ourselves. In fact, one way to consider the relationship between mindfulness and concentration is that mindfulness chooses the object and notices when attention goes astray, while concentration is what holds attention on that chosen object. Right Mindfulness, together with its partners Right Effort and Right Concentration, compose the section of the Eightfold Path related to *samadhi*. *Samadhi* is sometimes translated as "concentration," but its root meaning is "to combine, join, or put together." Buddhism inherited *samadhi* from Indian Vedic religion, in which the word indicates the union with a deity that one achieves through meditation. In modern Buddhism, we see the relationship between *samadhi* and nonduality— the one unified reality. We might think of Right Mindfulness as "awareness of awareness," working with Right Effort to put the teachings into practice and with Right Concentration to stay on task. This partnership creates the conditions for awakening to nonduality, a deep understanding that subject and object have always been joined and nonseparation has always been our true nature.

Now we can see that if Dogen's mindfulness is total immersion in the Way, it cannot be about focusing on one thing—a sensation, an activity, an object—to the exclusion of others. In fact, when we become preoccupied or obsessed with any one thing, it takes on such importance that it fills our whole view, pushing away the rest of this one unified reality and removing us to some abstract place. Focusing on the breath can make those sensations seem more important than any others in the body. Grasping a thought can make that thought the sum total of one's perceived experience, crowding out all of the other things that are actually going on. When we thus take things out of context, we don't have all of the available information, and we lose the very clarity we may have been trying to achieve.

Of course, the idea of just letting everything in at once can seem overwhelming. How are we to remain upright in this tidal wave of thoughts and feelings? How can we deal with all of it at the same time? How can that be mindfulness? We are accustomed to directing our attention to one thing after another, bouncing from image to idea to incident and working with each one in some way, deciding whether it's pleasant or not, useful or not, interesting or not. What if instead we let everything in without engaging with any particular element, without sorting, prioritizing, labeling, deciding, embroidering, or minimizing? We can give ourselves permission, even if just for a little while, not to process each incoming bit of data, but simply to be aware of its existence. What a relief!

Even zazen done in such a way as to try to block out noise or other distractions is not a manifestation of mindfulness. Any activity undertaken as a mindfulness practice is a gateway through which we enter so completely that there is no separation between ourselves and the activity, and no separation between ourselves, the activity, and everything else around us. When we stop directing and focusing our attention, attention arises of itself and excludes nothing. This is the self that has no beginning and no end.

What Is Mind, Really?

This brings us to the problem of mind. The words "mindful" and "mindfulness" imply that there is a mind that is full of separate elements—ideas, sensations, teachings, responsibilities, or potential dangers—and that ideally we carry these things at the forefront of our consciousness at all times. But this can't be what is really happening; not if nonseparation is the reality of our lives. There can't be a "mind" separate from the "things" of which it's supposed to be "full."

It's not the psychological "mind" we're talking about here, but *xin*. There's no one word in English that serves as a good translation for *xin*, so it's often called the "heart-mind." When the Chinese began translating sutras from Sanskrit, they used *xin* for Sanskrit terms like *citta*, *manas*, and *vijnana*. All of these refer to various consciousnesses in the Yogacara tradition, from which Zen can be said to derive, and in that way *xin* takes on a psychological association. However, *xin* was also used for the Sanskrit *hrdaya*, which can mean "heart," "center," or "essence." *Xin* as *citta* is in the realm of subject and object, a storehouse consciousness that contains karmic seeds, while *xin* as *hrdaya* means all dharmas (phenomena) in this one unified reality. (Okumura, par. 5)

When Dogen wrote about the mind in *Shobogenzo Sokushinzebutsu* (The Mind Itself is Buddha), he wrote about *xin* as *hrdaya*: "'The mind that has been authentically transmitted' is the one mind as all dharmas, and all dharmas as one mind. . . . An ancient patriarch said, 'What is fine, pure, and bright mind? It is mountains, rivers, and the earth, the sun, the moon, and stars.'" (Nishijima and Cross 1:69)

As my teacher, Shohaku Okumura, explained:

> Uchiyama Kosho Roshi often said that the xin used in Zen is not "psychological mind," but it is rather "life," which includes both subject and object. In the 1970s when I tried to explain this to an American friend, he was puzzled by the expression "psychological mind" and asked, "Is there such a thing as mind that is not psychological?" In Zen, I think we would say yes. (Okumura, par. 9)

If mind is everything we encounter, then Right Mindfulness is understanding there is no gap between ourselves and the rest of this one unified reality that transcends time and space.

Approaching The Sacred Space

While we're at it, we should understand what the original "foundations" of mindfulness are really all about. The Sanskrit word for which the English "foundation" is usually used is *upasthana*, which means something like "to draw near to something with respect." There is a sense of putting oneself in a sacred space and abiding there. When we combine it with *smrti*, "that which is remembered," we get *smrtiupasthana* or, in Pali, *satipattana*. However, the second part of the compound could also be *pasthana* (Pali: *paṭṭhana*), meaning "a starting point, basis, or foundation." Thus in English we sometimes see the Four Abodes of Mindfulness, and we sometimes see the Four Foundations.

How do we put ourselves into the sacred space of mindfulness and abide there? Although we may think of mindfulness as a sacred space, that doesn't mean it's a special state to be found somewhere other than here. If we're fully engaged in the mind that is all dharmas, the eternal now that continues in the ten directions, then all space and time is sacred space and time. We *draw near to all things with respect*, seeing them as they are, handling them with the care they deserve, not privileging any one dharma over another because all are equally empty. Abiding in that space, there is neither sacred nor mundane, nothing about which to become precious, and we see that we are not separate from anything in this one universal reality. Our practice is to remember and manifest the truth of this.

Dogen's Four Foundations

What does Dogen's Right Mindfulness look like in concrete terms? After all, mind-as-all-dharmas can seem rather vague and abstract, not something that's part of daily life. Let's look again at Dogen's four foundations of mindfulness from the *Eihei Koroku*, on which he elaborated in Shobogenzo *Sanjushichi-bon-bodai-bunpo* (Thirty Seven Elements of Bodhi).

Contemplating the body as a skin-bag

In contrast with Shakyamuni's instruction to contemplate the body as impure, Dogen tells us to see the body simply for the skin-bag it is, without judging it to be either pure or impure and without desiring to cast it in an unpleasant light to lessen our attachment to it (and, by extension, to the phenomenal world). Dogen sees the body as the ground of awakening, and thus indispensable. Without the body, he reminds us, there would be no practice, no preaching, no mindfulness itself. "When human beings become buddha, they utilize the human being to regulate the human being and to become buddha (Nishijima and Cross 4:4)."

The body is necessary for the kind of mindful, completely wholehearted daily activity that is the realization of our true nature, whether that activity is the formal practice Dogen detailed in his instructions for temple officers or the tasks of everyday twenty-first century Western life. However, becoming fixated on watching ourselves act is not the point of mindfulness, and fixation has the potential to increase our self-absorption. When we act selflessly with no gap—with no subject and object—that is exactly the complete manifestation of Buddha. In the instant of that manifestation, Dogen explains, trying to engage in any kind of additional mental "mindfulness" exercise is pointless. It would be an attempt to add an extra element to the reality of the body as the entire universe in the ten directions. Impossible! Mindfulness of the body is the body's own mindfulness practice, he points out, and thus there can be no separation between the body and the mind, the body and the universe, or practice and awakening.

Contemplating sensation as eating bowls

In the *Tenzo Kyokun* (Instructions for the Cook), Dogen recalls the old saying: "A monk's mouth is like an oven." Just as an oven does not resist or complain whether we put in cake, potatoes, or dog biscuits, a monk accepts whatever is put into his bowls. It begins during *takuhatsu* (alms rounds). When I was practicing in a temple in Japan, we would stop at a doorway and chant for the benefit of the people in the house or business; sometimes someone came out, and sometimes no one came out. A businesswoman might put a few yen in the bowl, or an old man might give some rice. A mother may give her little son an orange and show him how to offer it. No matter what we received, we chanted: "The virtue of the two kinds of offerings [material and dharma] is boundless; the perfection of generosity is completed and benefits all beings in the whole dharma world." No offering was scorned, and no offering was greeted with delight. All were equally accepted for the sake of the dharma.

When the offerings were prepared and served at mealtime, they were accepted with the recognition that they represented more than just the physical food in front of us—they represented the larger universe of labor, materials, and energy, and were received with equanimity. Sometimes, a local business owner would bring us all of his fresh tofu that was about to reach its sell-by date. It was perfectly fine, and we were happy to have it because our temple was at that time rather poor. However, we had to eat it all within a day or two to avoid having to throw it out, which was an unacceptable end for goods offered to a temple. Tofu was served at meal after meal until it was gone.

If we contemplate sensations as eating bowls, we accept the sensations with which we are presented, just as we accept what is put into our bowls. We take them all in, ignoring none whether pleasant, unpleasant, or neutral, and recognize that these too are part of the one unified reality. One way to consider these sensations is as suffering; unpleasant feelings are no fun, and pleasant feelings are doomed to fade away. Another way, Dogen suggests, is to consider them simply as elements to be accepted. They are not "ours," but neither are they outside somewhere, separate from us. Practicing with a body means practicing with the feeling that arises when the senses come in contact with sense objects. It's not necessary to decide how we feel about feelings; we can simply remain aware of them as they arise without obsessing or fixating on them and without analyzing them to invest them with special meaning. Obsession and analysis simply narrow our field of vision.

Contemplating mind as fences, walls, tiles and pebbles

If all dharmas are the one mind, then concrete manifestations of phenomenal reality like fences, walls, tiles, and pebbles are also mind. While the Buddha's instructions are to contemplate the mind as impermanent, Dogen uses one of his favorite metaphors for the world of form to show that mind is impermanent, dharmas are impermanent, and mind and dharmas are not separate. Our challenge is not to forget that everything we encounter is the one mind, and fences, walls, tiles, and pebbles are impermanent by nature just as mind is impermanent by nature. Mind is not somewhere else; it's right here among the forms that make up our daily existence. Coffee cups, smart phones, and running shoes are all mind, which means they are all impermanent.

Why do we care about this? What makes it more than a set of interesting mental gymnastics? Deeply understanding that all dharmas are mind and that mind is impermanent, we let go of the need to jump to conclusions about whether we like or dislike things and develop the ability to sustain some level of equanimity, even when faced with powerful events that have the potential to carry us away. The *Avatamsaka Sutra* says:

> In the sixth abode, the fulfillment of right mindfulness, there is no confusion about the inherent nature of things; meditating with right mindfulness, detaching from discrimination, one cannot

be moved by any god or man. Hearing praise or slander of the Buddhas or their teachings, of enlightening beings and the practices they perform, or that sentient beings are finite or infinite, defiled or undefiled, easy or hard to liberate, or that the cosmos is great or small, becomes or decays, or exists or does not, the mind is unmoved . . . . (Cleary 343)

Contemplating phenomena as old man Zhang drinking wine, old man Li getting drunk

Phenomena are non-substantial, yet they are interdependent elements of this one unified reality. Their nature is to arise and pass away; thus, they have no abiding self-nature that persists through time. Even so, their arising and passing away is not separate from the arising and passing away of all other phenomena. Dogen's quote about old man Zhang and old man Li comes from *Yunmen's Recorded Sayings*. He's using it here to show the interconnectedness of all beings, and that this interconnectedness is beyond the perception and workings of the intellect. How does it happen that when one person drinks sake, another feels the effects? How does it happen that we carry the dharma into the world without any intention of influencing others to practice, yet we hear from someone years later that watching how we handled the death of a parent inspired her to learn about Zen? We can't ignore phenomena simply because they are non-substantial. We have to go beyond their non-substantiality and bear in mind both that they are empty of any abiding self-nature, and that they are not separate from each other or ourselves, arising and passing away together in a vast interconnected system of causes and conditions.

OTHER MINDFULNESS PRACTICES

Dogen's consideration of mindfulness went beyond his repositioning of the Four Foundations. He included a long extract from the *Butsuhongyojikkyo* (Sutra of the Collected Stories of the Buddha's Deeds in Past Lives) in his *Shobogenzo*. *Ippyakuhachi homyomon* (One Hundred and Eight Gates of Dharma Illumination) mentions nine mindfulness-related practices related to this discussion (Nishijima and Cross 343-350).

Mindfulness of Buddha, Dharma and Sangha

For early Buddhists, recollecting the virtues of the Tathagata, including his awakening, knowledge, conduct, expertise in the ways of the world, and skill as a teacher, allowed them to avoid being overcome by passion, aversion, or delusion. Calming the body, they were better able to concentrate on the dharma and experience the joy and rapture that naturally arose. This recollection was to be done not only on the cushion, but throughout the day while walking, standing, sitting, lying down, working or resting.

The same effect could be experienced by recollecting the dharma as well spoken by the Buddha: timeless, pertinent, and to be verified for oneself by one's own tangible, personal experience. Similarly, one recollected the sangha as comprising those who have practiced well, straightforwardly, methodically, and masterfully, and as representing the incomparable field of merit, being made up of practitioners worthy of gifts, hospitality, offerings, and respect.

Complete immersion in these Three Treasures allows us to reflect them perfectly, without gaps or additions. When it is awakening that is awakening, rather than we who are awakening, Buddha is manifested purely. When the universe operates through us without obstruction, the view of the dharma is unrestricted. When there is no separation between ourselves and the sangha, there is no chance for wobbling and falling off the path.

Mindfulness of generosity—no expectation of reward

Early Buddhists recalled that in the midst of human society defiled by greed, they had the good fortune to cultivate generosity, openhandedness, magnanimity, responsiveness, and delight in giving alms. The joy that arose from practicing in this way was its own reward.

Wholehearted engagement in giving means that giving is just giving. As exemplified by *takuhatsu* practice, there is no self, no giver, no receiver, no gift, and no thought of reward arises. In the one unified reality, there is no giving and no not-giving, because everything is already complete.

Mindfulness of precepts—fulfilling all vows

While there is separation in our day-to-day existence, we need the ethical guidelines of the precepts as guideposts on the path. When we see through separation, no thought of unwholesome action arises, and we don't break precepts. It's no longer a question of watching ourselves to prevent unwholesome thoughts and actions. There is no one vowing, no one breaking vows, no one fulfilling vows. There is simply the complete and skillful operating of the one unified reality. When we wholeheartedly engage in functioning within that reality, the small self drops away, and effective action for the benefit of all beings occurs naturally.

Mindfulness of the heavens—giving rise to wide and big mind

Early Buddhists brought to mind not just the heavens, but also the beings that occupied them—the devas. They recalled that the conviction, virtue, learning, generosity and discernment of the myriad devas was present in themselves as well, and on that basis they enjoyed liberation from the three poisons, calmed themselves, developed concentration, cleansed the mind of defilements, and experienced joy.

Bringing to mind inspiring elements such as the Three Treasures or the devas was not meant to be a practice in itself, however. Once the experience of the element had dispelled fear and produced calm and pleasure, the practitioner was to withdraw his mind from the object of inspiration and abandon directed thought and discrimination.

Mindfulness thorough performance of work

Mindful work is work done without a doer, a task, or an outcome. When we are not separate from action, we perform thoroughly—we do all that is necessary with nothing extra and nothing left out. No matter whether the task at hand is simple, like putting books back on a shelf, or more complex, like figuring out why the car has suddenly begun to make a high-pitched whine, we can do it seamlessly. That doesn't mean we do it to the exclusion of awareness that the bookend is about to tip over or that a toddler on a trike has just pedaled up behind the back bumper. As Dogen teaches in the *Tenzo Kyokun*, each item with which we're working needs to be handled carefully and with understanding about its relationship to all other dharmas. He quotes an old teacher: "When steaming rice, regard the pot as your own head; when washing rice, know that the water is your own life (Leighton and Okumura 36)."

Years ago I heard a story about Zen students who worked in a business started and run by their center. They were convinced that their practice required them to do everything slowly and deliberately, carefully placing each object and product just so, and were oblivious to the growing line of impatient customers waiting for service. This is not Dogen's mindfulness.

Mindful does not mean slow. Mindfulness has no set speed. It just does what needs to be done, in full awareness of everything around it.

The power of mindfulness—taking responsibility

When we remember the reality of our interconnection with all dharmas, we avoid becoming dazzled by the personalities of others, forgetting to take responsibility for our own thoughts and actions and their outcomes. Otherwise, "It wasn't my fault," we tell ourselves later. "I just went along with what everyone else was doing. It wasn't my idea."

This is what my dharma grandfather, Kodo Sawaki, called "group stupidity." He had little patience for people who went along with the crowd and abrogated their personal responsibility, or for those who created strategies to lead others astray in the name of money, power, or fame. He wrote:

> When people are alone, they're not so bad. However, when a group forms, paralysis occurs; people become totally foolish and cannot distinguish good from bad. Their minds are numbed by the group. Because of their desire to belong and even to lose themselves, some pay membership fees. Others work on advertising to attract people and intoxicate them for some political, spiritual or commercial purpose. I keep some distance from society, not to escape it but to avoid this kind of paralysis. To practice zazen is to become free of this group stupidity. (Uchiyama 23)

Numbing the mind, intentionally or not, turns off our ability to see the consequences of what we do and the effect of our action (or inaction) across this one unified reality. If we're really mindful, awake and aware, we prevent unwholesome states from arising, unwholesome actions from being carried out, and unwholesome effects from harming beings.

Mindfulness and Memory

The memory element of mindfulness is vitally important to Soto Zen practice. According to Dogen, it's what Right Mindfulness is all about. In the *Hachidainingaku* (The Eight Truths of Great People), he defines Right Mindfulness as simply to keep the dharma and not to lose it. Not losing the dharma means not losing touch with reality, not forgetting our true nature and the true nature of everything we encounter, not forgetting our vow to wake up and save all beings. No matter the circumstances in which we find ourselves, we remember that we are Buddha and we are not swept away. "When your mindfulness is solid," Dogen explains, "you will not be harmed even if you go into the midst of the robbers of the five sense desires. It is like wearing armor and going into a battlefield, so there is nothing to be afraid of (Tanahashi 272)."

This teaching originates with Asvagosha: "He who has established mindfulness as a guard at the doors of his mind cannot be overpowered by the passions, as a well guarded city cannot be overcome by the enemy (Nyanaponika 215)." For early Buddhists, the protective nature of mindfulness was related to being on guard for the arising of unwholesome states. For later practitioners like Dogen, the point perhaps is that, when we forget about the essential teachings of this tradition, we create the gap that leaves us open to the suffering caused by craving and aversion. As soon as there is separation, there are sense organs contacting objects and giving rise to the five skandhas and to birth and death. Bearing in mind what the Buddhas and ancestors taught, always recalling that we are not separate from this one unified reality, we are safe from being robbed of our tranquility by the demands of our senses. When we maintain mindfulness, we are impervious to attack by hindrances because there is no gap through which they can enter.

There are a number of ways to pull this protection more tightly around us. One is chanting, and *nen* appears in several of the most familiar Soto Zen chants. When chanting, we invoke or call to mind various significant bodhisattvas and ancestors such that their presence leads and inspires us, reminding us of our bodhisattva vows. *Cho nen Kanzeon; bo nen Kanzeon*, goes the Enmei Jiku Kannon Gyo. *Nen nen ju shin ki; nen nen fu ri shin*. (In the morning think of Kanzeon; in the evening think of Kanzeon. Thought after thought arises from mind; thought after thought is not separate from mind.) This thinking is not an intellectual activity so much as an abiding with Kanzeon, not forgetting our aspiration to free ourselves and others from suffering right in the middle of this phenomenal world. This mindfulness is itself the activity of *xin* (in this case, the Japanese *shin*), the heart-mind; it arises naturally from the interdependent network of empty phenomena, and is not separate.

Likewise, the various *nenju* (remembrance chanting) and *nenki* (memorials) that are part of life in a training temple are opportunities to strengthen mindfulness. On days ending in 3 or 8 we reenact our entry into the training temple in a ceremony called *Sampachi Nenju* and recall the Ten Names of Buddha as we renew our intention to train, inviting Buddhas and bodhisattvas to be with us in memory and spirit as we practice. The *Gyouhatsu Nenju* that begins formal meals also includes the Ten Names: "In the midst of the three treasures, which verify our understanding, entrusting ourselves to the sangha, we recall (*nen*) . . . ." In fact, the meal chant includes a summary of the Buddha's life and teachings, and each mealtime is an excellent opportunity to bring back to mind the basics of our tradition and go forth carrying them afresh.

Thus we can consider mindfulness as a practice of remembrance—remembering the tradition and its teachings, remembering our vows and our commitment to practice, remembering the Buddhas and ancestors who have gone before us making a path for us to follow, remembering the aspects of our lives and experience that we'd rather ignore, remembering that reality is not what we think it is. Right Mindfulness is all-inclusive, encompassing everything in this boundless reality.

Of course, if we become precious about our mindfulness, we're sunk. Mindfulness becomes just another idea, something we use to write stories about ourselves or to achieve some worldly purpose. As Gudo Wafu Nishijima points out: "If someone in Buddhism reveres mindfulness, we should clearly recognize that he or she can never [be] a Buddhist at all (Nishijima 24)." Mindfulness is not special, not an extraordinary state that we achieve through zazen or mental exercises. If we're making some extraordinary effort to maintain something called "mindfulness," we've missed the mark. Right Mindfulness is not something that exists only in special conditions. It arises naturally of itself when we see deeply into the nature of this moment and understand that there never was a separation between ourselves and anything else.

THE MINDFULNESS BACKLASH

There's enough buzz about "mindfulness" in pop culture today that there is also a "mindfulness industry" and a "mindfulness backlash." Books, recordings, classes, apps, all the accoutrements of popular mindfulness are suddenly available for purchase. However, more and more consumers are finding themselves frustrated and anxious as a result of their attempts to become mindful, rather than peaceful and relaxed as they had hoped. One newspaper columnist wrote:

I inevitably wind up cursing my brain and its runaway thoughts, because 20 minutes of fidgeting won't deliver the promised fruits of meditative labours: a serene disposition, increased mental clarity and a compassionate soul. By the time I crossly tear off my headphones or shove the yoga mat in the corner, these rewards have never felt further from my reach. I've wasted precious time that could have been spent on something I love, and I've failed, again, at something seemingly everyone else finds both effortless and effective. (Hart, par. 3-4)

Popular mindfulness meditation is often characterized as being "derived" from Buddhism and that "derivation" is precisely the problem. Somehow, somebody got the idea that mindfulness is a short cut to feeling happy, confident, and in control by "zoning out," making thoughts (particularly stressful or confused thoughts) disappear, and creating a blank mental canvas. This, of course, is exactly the opposite of Dogen's mindfulness that is one hundred percent engagement with the world, including the thoughts and feelings that become more evident during zazen.

Beginning meditators often report that their minds seem busier than before they started sitting, which sometimes leads to increased stress and self-doubt. Teachers reply that it isn't that there are more thoughts than ever before, but that the practitioner has gained a much more realistic view of the daily, ongoing busyness of the mind and is now in a position to practice effectively with that reality. "Zoning out," escaping from life or suppressing thought, is not mindfulness, and comparing one's practice with that of one's friends is not a useful measure of validity. "Everyone but me seems to be enjoying and benefiting from mindfulness activities" is simply another mental construct. It's not easy to come face to face with the thoughts that arise; it is easy to find an excuse to stop practicing. It's especially easy to abandon the whole thing when we set inappropriate and unrealistic goals for our mindfulness such as instant serenity, compassion, and joy.

Popular mindfulness has been removed from its Buddhist context such that it appeals to a broad audience that may be uncomfortable with organized religion. It's been further surrounded with scientific discussion that appeals to those who may be looking for a "rational" practice. This type of meditation does give some people what they want; others, however, find it unsatisfying or even unsettling. When removed from its Buddhist context, popular mindfulness lacks the foundation of the entire dharma system, the elements of which are designed to support each other. Without observation of the precepts, we create suffering and confusion for ourselves and others, making it difficult to concentrate and settle into practice. Without insight into the nature of reality, we go on creating and recreating the "self," using mindfulness activities as self-help techniques to try to become people we like better. When concentration becomes fixation, we lose our balance and can be overwhelmed by a narrow view that privileges one sensation, thought or experience over the rest of our existence.

It's very difficult to sustain a meditation practice without including the rest of the dharma support structure in our lives. Can mindfulness be divorced from its close partners, Right Effort and Right Concentration, or from the rest of the Eightfold Path for that matter, and remain an effective support for our awakening? No wonder that, without guidance on how to dispel misconception and how to live ethically and wisely, after just twenty minutes a beginning practitioner might feel hopeless, succumb to the backlash, and give up.

As we've seen, Dogen's mindfulness is one in which there is simply full engagement with the moment. There is no outside part of ourselves watching what we are doing with some intention or strategy or agenda. There is no idea of being morally right or wrong, because Right Mindfulness transcends such distinctions. Out of mindfulness—complete nonseparation with all dharmas—wholesomeness naturally arises without the need for thinking about it. The mind that abides nowhere can abide everywhere—not fixed on any one thing, but taking in the whole interconnected system that is the universe.

The final mindfulness-related gate in the *Ippakuhachi homyomon* says: "Right mindfulness is a gate of Dharma illumination; for [with it] we do not consider all dharmas intellectually (Nishijima and Cross 4:351)." The mind-that-is-all-dharmas is not the intellectual, discriminating, psychological mind, but the functioning of the vast interconnected network of impermanent elements that make up a complete reality. This reality is beyond the intellect; thus with Right Mindfulness, we see beyond the intellect to the reality of our lives. We recall the teachings of those who've walked the path before us. We renew our aspiration and intention. We remember our true place in that reality.

Works cited

Cleary, Thomas F., trans. *The Flower Ornament Scripture: A Translation of the Avatamsaka Sutra.* Boulder: Shambhala, 1984.

Hart, Anna. *"Mindfulness Backlash: Could Meditation Be Bad for Your Health?"* The Telegraph. Telegraph Media Group, 24 Oct. 2015. Web. 2 Nov. 2015.

Leighton, Taigen Daniel and Shohaku Okumura, trans. "Tenzo Kyokun (Instructions for the Cook). *Dogen's Extensive Record: a Translation of the Eihei Koroku.* New York: Wisdom, 2010.

---. *Dogen's Pure Standards for the Zen Community: a Translation of the Eihei Shingi.* Albany, NY: State U of New York, 1996.

Nishijima, Gudo Wafu and Chodo Cross, trans. "Ippyakuhachi-homyomon (One Hundred and Eight Gates of Dharma Illumination)." *Shōbōgenzō : The True Dharma-eye Treasury; (Taishō Volume 82, Number 2582).* Berkeley, CA: Numata Center for Buddhist Transl. and Research, 2008.

---. "Sanjushichi-bon-bodai-bunpo (Thirty Seven Elements of Bodhi)." Ibid.

---. "Sokuishinzebutsu (The Mind Itself Is Buddha)." Ibid.

Nishijima, Gudo Wafu. "On Mindfulness." *Dogen Sangha Blog.* 24 May 2008. Web. 3 Nov. 2015.

Nyanaponika, Himi. *Satipatthāna: The Heart of Buddhist Meditation: A Handbook of Mental Training Based on the Buddha's Way of Mindfulness.* Kandy: Buddhist Publications Society, 2005.

Okumura, Shohaku. "Dharma Dictionary: Kokoro." *Lion's Roar.* 1 Sept. 2005. Web. 2 Nov. 2015. <http://www.lionsroar.com/dharma-dictionary-kokoro/>

Tanahashi, Kazuaki. "Hachidainingaku (The Eight Truths of Great People)." *Enlightenment Unfolds: The Essential Teachings of Zen Master Dogen.* Boston: Shambhala, 1999.

Uchiyama, Kosho and Shohaku Okumura. *The Zen Teaching of Homeless Kodo.* Boston: Wisdom, 2014.

CHAPTER 8

Right Samadhi or Concentration
Pat Enkyo O'Hara

O ver two thousand years ago, in India, a woman follower of Shakyamuni wrote a verse:

> I cultivated a state of mind
> That depends on nothing else and cannot be measured,
> I became focused, collected.
> I am free, and I will always be completely free. (Hallisey 63)

This woman, called Sona, describes a "state of mind" that sounds centered and composed and at the same time unrestrained. When she says that it "depends on nothing else," it's as if she experiences a quality of mind that doesn't hinge on her life situation, her past, or on whether she is feeling good or bad, happy or sad. Instead, it is a way of being that renders her centered and at one with her wholeness, just as it is. As she plainly says, she is "free." It is quite an expansive and remarkable statement, given the times and her situation as a female follower of Shakyamuni and mother of ten.

Now, when I go to my cushion to sit meditation (zazen) I am often still overflowing with various thoughts, ideas, things to do, and sometimes, as I sit down, find my posture, regulate my breathing, place my tongue against my front teeth, I am still chatting with myself about this and that. This is when I say to myself, "Stop talking." When I stop talking to myself, I begin to sink into a flow of experience that really has no description; it simply *is*, is flow itself. It is moment-to-moment aliveness, a more spacious experience of myself as an element in the life of all Life. Recently, after zazen, I wrote,

> Sitting quietly,
> I meet myself,
> Stripped of words and ideas,
> Just this, just this.
> nothing is left out!

Thousands of years apart, two women drink of the same river, the healing waters of wholesome concentration, of samadhi. What is it? Has it changed?

My Manhattan neighborhood is changing so fast, it is hard to recognize the old haunts: they aren't there anymore. The jazz clubs, the sleepy bodegas, the pocket parks are gone, replaced by so many banks and drugstores and ever-escalating apartment buildings. Because I love this neighborhood, I want to care for it, to preserve what's valuable, and yet also to allow new growth to blossom. I want to ensure that we keep some sunlight, air, and that extraordinary cast-iron building, but also room for more bicycles, young people, poor people, new businesses, architecture, and fresh ways of seeing the urban experience. I keep reminding myself of the truth of impermanence: that we are all in a boat flowing down an ever-moving river of change. As Dogen said, we may not realize it, but what's in the boat is also changing.

This too, is true of our beloved Buddhist canon and its view of samadhi. The earliest teachings that we now have, the Pali Sutras, first written down around the first century, form the foundation for the many strands of Buddhist practice that have evolved in multiple forms in Asia, and now in the Western world. Imagine the myriad evolutions of meaning and use and context as these early writings poured into Southeast Asia, into the cultures of China, Japan, Korea, and now the West, in Europe, and Northern and Southern Americas. This cultural and spatial transformation of the teachings is also affected by the inexorable flow of time and generational change. How *anything* is interpreted is so modulated by indigenous culture, accidental history, and the unexplained, that we must be careful not to fixate on any one meaning of samadhi.

What's more, the word "samadhi" is old! It predates Buddhism and appears in the earliest Upanishads, the Maitrayaniya. Samadhi is also integral to the teachings of Yoga, Jainism, Hinduism and Sikhism. It appears in shamanistic works, in the many Buddhist traditions, and is a rather common contemporary logo for commercial products: candles, blankets, pillows, teas, clothes.

Yes, indeed, samadhi can mean many things, depending on where and when it is employed!

As the eighth element of the Eightfold Path, *Samma Samadhi* is typically translated these days into English as "Right Concentration" or "Wholesome Concentration" or tellingly, just "Concentration." The

Sanskrit *samadhi* customarily refers simply to meditation or contemplation, and its etymology carries the sense of "a bringing together," or "bringing together completely" or "one-pointedness"—a kind of focus, a gathering in of disparate parts. The Chinese translators sometimes transliterated the sound *samadhi* as *san mai* (三昧), and other times replaced it with *ding*, 定, which means "fixity." The character *ding* shows a roof over the character *stop*, thus emphasizing a protective, immovable structure sheltering the energy of "stop." To "stop" the motion of mind—it seems such a fitting loan word!

Likewise, if we consider that the English word to "concentrate" originally meant to "bring something to the center," and later came to imply "distilling by removing the inessential," and finally "to focus one's attention," we can form a mental map of this word "concentration" as it is used to translate *samadhi*: we bring our mind to the center, we let the incidental thoughts drop away, we align and stabilize, we stop the scattering—we focus.

As is true of the other elements in the Path, it is important to remember that concentration without the qualifier "right" or "wholesome" can be a very different thing. Just as morality or speech or thinking can be twisted into sinister uses, so too can concentration. The concentrated focus of a vengeful, selfish, or delusional person may involve sharp attentiveness to one point, but can hardly be construed as a "wholesome" use of concentration. In fact, now that "meditation" has become fashionable and touted to be useful for optimizing work and gain in the marketplace, many American Buddhists have voiced ethical concerns that the teaching of meditation is often not accompanied by a structure of ethical teachings. On the other hand, others argue that any immersion in meditation practice is likely to lead to greater self-awareness and wisdom and a net "good" for society. Nevertheless, it seems to me that discerning wholesome and unwholesome uses of all the elements of the Eightfold Path remains an ongoing responsibility of those of us who teach the Dharma.

As I mentioned above, when we are in the midst of change (and we always are, whether we realize it or not), we have a responsibility to preserve the old that is worthwhile and also embrace the new that can serve what is good. We can drink deeply from the past teachings on concentration and rely on them to guide us, as well as employ technology and science when they offer skillful and nourishing aids to concentration. Scientific research is broadening acceptance and understanding of the power of meditative absorption, leading to skillful interventions for education and medicine, as well as for ordinary meditators. Digital and communications technologies serve to introduce dispersed individuals to Dharma teachings as well as provide new ways to monitor their meditative practices. In this way, we can encourage the spread of concentration practice, its inherent steadiness, and its relevance, braided together with the other seven elements of the Eightfold Path, as an antidote to the distractions and unthinking conduct of people who need refuge.

Perhaps the earliest written description of the Eightfold Path's "Right Concentration" can be found in the *Samyutta Nikaya*. Here, in Bhikkhu Bodhi's translation, is a kind of "origin" text:

> And what, monks, is right concentration? Here, monks, secluded from sensual pleasures, secluded from unwholesome states, a monk enters and dwells in the first *jhana*, which is accompanied by thought and examination, with rapture and happiness born of seclusion. With the subsiding of thought and examination, he enters and dwells in the second *jhana*, which has internal confidence and unification of mind, is without thought and examinations and has rapture and happiness born of concentration. With the fading away as well of rapture, he dwells equanamous and, mindful and clearly comprehending, he experiences happiness with the body; he enters and dwells in the third *jhana* of which the noble ones declare: "He is equanamous, mindful, one who dwells happily." With the abandoning of pleasure and pain, and with the previous passing away of joy and dejection, he enters and dwells in the fourth *jhana*, which is neither painful nor pleasant and includes the purification of mindfulness by equanimity. This is called right concentration. (Bodhi SN45:8, V8-10)

The Pali word *jhana* above corresponds to the Sanskrit *dhyana* that, in turn, we know as "Chan" or "Zen" and is often translated simply as meditation. We could summarize this description of entering mediation as a concentrative state involving increasingly deeper levels of awareness: appreciating a quiet environment, dropping thoughts, immersion in concentration, abandoning pain and pleasure, and culminating in equanimity. It is more a "description" of an experience (rapture, happiness, confidence, unification of mind, equanamous and mindful) than it is a specific instruction of a practice to attain such a state of concentration.

But how we long for a recipe, a clear instruction on how to enter into right concentration! As you might imagine, there are as many systems of such instruction as there are streams of the Dharma. Depending on what school, what time period, what language and culture, the practice instruction will vary. Later texts in many of the Buddhist traditions are highly codified, prescriptive instructions, delineating a step-by-step methodology for attaining progressive grades of samadhi.

My own experience with concentration comes from my American Zen Buddhist tradition, a form brought to this country by Maezumi Roshi from Japan, bringing together elements from the Soto as well as the Rinzai schools. (I've included at the end of this chapter a brief contemporary instruction for zazen that we use in my Zen Center.) We were taught to assume a balanced, upright posture, to begin by counting our outbreaths to ten, and back to one, until our concentration was focused enough to stop counting. We might then maintain attention on our breath until we achieved sufficient focus to drop any object of attention, and simply "sit zazen." As one of our treasured, yet terse, meditation instructions has it: "Having adjusted your body in this manner, take a breath and exhale fully, then sway your body to left and right. Now sit steadfastly and think not-thinking. How do you think not-thinking? Beyond thinking. This is the essential art of zazen (Tanahashi 5)."

It is hard to get our minds around the concept of "beyond thinking"—especially when we are thinking about it! Accustomed to "doing," to grasping for something other than what's here, we have to learn to drop into the stream of breath, no longer counting it, but being it. The thinking, the intentionality drops away, and we can simply enjoy the ebb and flow of samadhi: this is "beyond thinking." It is more like riding on a slow-moving current in a broad river.

In my first immersion during a long retreat, I tasted a quality of body and mind that was deep and soothing, a stilling of the constant rush and scattering of emotion and intellect that most of us humans experience without pause. But I could not explain it, nor could I very succinctly detail its progression, and I certainly did not understand it. It reminds me of a telling remark of Gertrude Stein's. When she was asked how people could possibly understand the modernist opera she wrote with Virgil Thomson, she replied: "By understanding you mean you can talk about it in the way you have a habit of talking. But I mean you enjoy it and if you enjoy it, then you understand it (qtd. in Cowles, par. 3)." Stein tellingly reminds us that enjoyment is a different way of understanding, one that embodies our physical and emotional experience rather than our habitual verbal and cognitive patterns of "understanding."

The "enjoyment" of samadhi resonates even in the often rather austere early scriptures quoted above, with "rapture" and "happiness" so prominent. It is that enjoyment we hear in my own tradition's core teacher, the brilliant Eihei Dogen (1200-1250), when he echoes an even earlier Chinese Zen teacher, Ch'ang-lu Tsung-tse (c. mid-11th century), saying that the practice of samadhi is the dharma gate of enjoyment and ease: "Extolling it, an ancestor said, 'Zazen is the dharma gate of enjoyment and ease.' Thus, we know that sitting practice, among the four bodily presences, is the way of enjoyment and ease (Tanahashi 1:41)."

Enjoyment and ease are qualities impossible to experience when we are grasping for something that we think is outside our reach. One of the most difficult challenges to new practitioners is exactly that striving to "get" or "achieve" samadhi as they inexorably move away from it. Often, this desire to attain creates suffering and tension for the meditator, far from ease or enjoyment. Instead, a more settled energy is needed.

Recently, I was scheduled to give a talk on Mother's Day, and it occurred to me that the qualities we associate with mothers and babies, the reassuring sense of being held, unified, soothed and contained, the feeling of utter intimacy, are also qualities of our enjoyment of samadhi. With delight, I discovered Dogen's line in his *Shobogenzo* essay on the "Thirty-seven Wings of Enlightenment," "The power of samadhi is like a child having a mother or a mother having a child. It is like a child having a child, or a mother having a mother (Tanahashi 2:255)."

Like much of Dogen's writing, this short phrase evokes an ever-changing flow of intimacy: the relational field of mother and child, and also the experience of child as mother, and mother as child, each to themselves and to the other. Notice that Dogen is pointing to the "power" of samadhi, its strength that arises through the intimate functions of closeness, soothing, and holding. Isn't it this quality of samadhi, of concentration, that softens us and encourages us to continue our meditation practice and to offer it to others? Indeed, it may be this particular quality of samadhi that opens the door to service in the world. This ability to quiet our minds in safety, to allow ourselves to rest on the breast of life, surely encourages us to offer such compassion to others.

In another fascicle of *Shobogenzo*, "Ocean Mudra Samadhi," Dogen alludes to this connection between samadhi and the compassionate service of Avalokitesvara:

> Samadhi is actualization; it is expression. It is the time of night when a hand is reaching back, groping for a pillow. When the hand reaches back for a pillow at night, this groping is not limited to thousands and millions of eons, but is 'I am always in the ocean expounding the wondrous Lotus Sutra.' " (Tanahashi 1:489)

The "hand groping for a pillow" refers to a beloved story of two Dharma brothers, Yun Yen and Dao Wu, and their dialogue about the functioning of compassion:

> Yun Yen asked Dao Wu, "How does Bodhisattva of Compassion use all those many hands and eyes?"
> Dao Wu answered, "It is like someone in the middle of the night reaching behind his head for the pillow." (Cleary 489)

Consider how Dogen interprets this "middle of the night" as a samadhi that leads to activity. Rather than a quietistic state of lifelessness, it is a place from which we can spontaneously act and express as does Avalokitesvara, the one who "sees and hears the sounds" of the world and uses her many hands and eyes to relieve suffering. Avalokitesvara expresses and actualizes the activity of samadhi by expounding the teaching of the *Lotus Sutra* in the "ocean"—the ocean of samadhi. This teaching of the *Lotus Sutra* is not focused on individual attainment, but rather the responsibility to assist all beings to realize their buddha nature.

What strikes me is the dynamic nature of Dogen's description of samadhi: actualization, expression, reaching, groping, expounding—these are not the "ashes and dead wood" that Zen meditators from time to time have been accused of embodying. Yet, because Dogen often emphasizes this liveliness of samadhi, it is likely that he is pointing to a hazard: quietism, blankness, or what some of my contemporaries call "Zen Zombies"—meditators who demonstrate an apathetic and unresponsive stance to every encounter.

The psychotherapist John Welwood popularized the term "spiritual bypassing" to illustrate the psychologically unhealthy ways that meditation can be used to numb, to hide, to lose oneself in quietude. In an interview in Tricycle magazine, Welwood explained,

> Spiritual bypassing is a term I coined to describe a process I saw happening in the Buddhist community I was in, and also in myself. Although most of us were sincerely trying to work on our-

selves, I noticed a widespread tendency to use spiritual ideas and practices to sidestep or avoid facing unresolved emotional issues, psychological wounds, and unfinished developmental tasks.

When we are spiritually bypassing, we often use the goal of awakening or liberation to rationalize what I call *premature transcendence*: trying to rise above the raw and messy side of our humanness before we have fully faced and made peace with it. And then we tend to use absolute truth to disparage or dismiss relative human needs, feelings, psychological problems, relational difficulties, and developmental deficits. (Welwood 1)

Hiding one's real needs and feelings often results in mounting internal tension and occasional antisocial conduct. It isn't surprising that vulnerable seekers in pursuit of release from personal suffering are likely to seek a cozy hiding place in samadhi. In their need to find security and relief from the pressure of unexamined experiences, they may gravitate to the seamless quality of samadhi. Thinking that samadhi is abstract and apart from their actual life, they may misinterpret the instruction to focus on the breath and think that it means to dissociate from their feelings, or that to experience numbness is samadhi, or that one's feelings are not "enlightened." This misinterpretation of the teachings is not new, and, as in the past, it is the responsibility of teachers and community to notice this tendency and to address it. If the community of practitioners is alert to this tendency, they often teach one another through informal back-and-forth before and after meditation practice. In many contemporary Zen Centers, there is a kind of lightness and "anti-holy" mood that often serves to interrupt the bypassing syndrome. As a matter of fact, in my experience, it is not at all unusual these days for a Dharma Teacher to ask, "Are you in therapy? Have you sought help?"

Eight hundred years before Welwood's observation, in a remote mountain monastery, Dogen seems to point to the same danger; if we are lost in a narcotized trance, deadened to life, we won't extend our arm in the middle of the night to offer compassionate relief to ourselves or others, to use those "many hands and eyes" of the Bodhisattva of Compassion, to offer the teachings, to offer support, service, and expression to life and living beings.

Just as Dogen often emphasized that meditation practice, zazen, is not a path to enlightenment, but actually is the manifestation of enlightenment, so too, the expression of samadhi rests in our ordinary lives.

There is the story of Yunmen who was asked by his disciple, "What is every atom samadhi?" Yunmen replied, "Rice in the bowl, water in the bucket." Imagine the situation, an eager beginner, filled with the excitement of the prospect of experiencing samadhi as it is described in Chapter Twelve of the *Flower Ornament Scripture*, how Bodhisattvas enter "every atom samadhi:"

> They enter concentration on one atom,
> And accomplish concentration on all atoms,
> And yet that particle doesn't increase,
> In one are manifest inconceivable lands. (Cleary 339)

With its characteristic florid descriptions, the *Flower Ornament Scripture* paints an image resembling space travel, in which the Bodhisattvas, upon entering this "every atom concentration," visit many lands, have spiritual powers, and exhibit brilliance and lights. And how does our Yunmen respond to this question? "Rice in the bowl, water in the bucket." Here is "every atom samadhi." Yunmen moves us, from words and images and fantastical imagination, back to this moment, this life, as "every atom samadhi"—nothing missing, nothing bypassed, our ordinary life.

This year, a few months after talking about the maternal nature of samadhi, I found myself preparing to give a talk on Father's Day, and it was Yunmen's "rice in the bowl, water in the bucket" response that brought to mind another aspect of what I think of as the characteristics of the "Samadhi Family": the paternal qualities usually associated with the father archetype—accountability, rigor, discipline, protection, dealing with the external world. Yunmen's insistence that samadhi can be found in our rice bowl, in our everyday sustenance, brings the monk, and us, back to our real life as it is lived. In this response, the power of samadhi, of concentration, rests in the fruits of attention, whether to one's breath or one's bowl, whether to one's habit of mind or one's method of interaction with the world. Yunmen reminds us that our practice of samadhi is not an abstract or hypnotic idea, but this life itself. Every atom includes every thing. Food in the bowl nourishes life; water in the bucket stewards the planet. Samadhi and this daily ordinary life are not two.

These days we are besieged with notices of our rising distractibility and loss of focus. Actually, I don't know if our contemporary life with its electronic devices, multiple roles, and visual and auditory distractions is really any more demanding of our attention than life a thousand years ago, when the time and labor-saving technologies we take for granted did not exist. In point of fact, many ancient writings deplore the ease with which we humans fall into distraction and into repetitive patterns of thought. A thousand years ago, the Chinese Zen Master, Hongzhi (1091-1157), wrote of samadhi:

> Contemplating your own authentic form is how to contemplate Buddha. If you can experience yourself without distractions, simply surpass partiality and go beyond conceptualizing. All buddhas and all minds reach the essential without duality. (Leighton 10)

And,

> You must purify, cure, grind down, or brush away all the tendencies you have fabricated into apparent habits. Then you can reside in the clear circle of brightness. (4)

And,

> To gain such steadiness you must completely withdraw from the invisible pounding and weaving of your ingrained ideas. If you want to be rid of this invisible turmoil, you must just sit through it and let go of everything. (21)

Indeed, we have to, as Hongzhi says, "grind down and brush away" our habits of mind, lazy ways of thinking, the old stories we tell ourselves. When we are wrapped in outmoded thoughts and ways of perceiving reality, we limit our response to ever-changing circumstances, and our ability to respond to them with compassion and wisdom; it isn't easy to even recognize that we are operating from old habits and ideas. We need to call up in ourselves some of the qualities we associate with fathering: a responsibility to ourselves, a sense of rigor, using discipline to train our minds, being accountable to ourselves for the seamlessness of our meditation practice. It is the "stop talking" I alluded to when describing my own process of zazen.

We can summon the qualities of discipline and self-accountability to help us navigate the struggle to let go of our habitual thinking. I think of these as attributes of the father archetype, the one who teaches us how to do things, how to manage our relations with the external world. It is the father energy that protects us and shows us how to protect ourselves, using our own internal discipline and rigor so that we may enter the realm of concentration, of samadhi.

Not surprisingly, when I think of the "Mother Samadhi" who holds us tenderly in her arms and the "Father Samadhi" who keeps us accountable, I want to include "Baby Samadhi." In ancient China, there was an expression associated with a Zen student who had first tasted samadhi, who had entered into a state of deep concentration: a newborn baby. It is the aspect of samadhi that is innocent, playful, fresh, and lively. If we listen to Hongzhi's instruction to grind down our habitual way of thinking, and thus free ourselves, we may encounter this spontaneous and fresh aspect of samadhi.

It bears repeating that, when we first begin our meditation practice, we may think that we're going to obtain something, we're going to go and get something that will make our life better; actually, what we learn is that we are letting go of what impedes us. We begin to—in a current phrase—"de-clutter" our minds. We let go of a lot of the old baggage that we've been dragging around that prevents us from encountering our lives from a fresh point of view. Instead of the outmoded, no longer helpful voices railing about our personal lives, about our social relations, and about the world around us, we find ourselves experiencing the world, others, and ourselves differently. What has happened?

As we begin to practice more frequently, we recognize that these old ideas do just drop away, and we're able to be fresh and alive and discover creative, new ways of working with ourselves, others, and the world: new techniques, new stratagems. We're not locked into the old rhetoric of ourselves and others.

This can be seen as experiencing the benefits of "Baby Samadhi," of the freshness and innocence, the joy and openness, the aliveness and immediacy of a baby. Next time you encounter a baby, look at the eyes going this way and that, the soft round facial expressions, the wide-open face and eyes; listen to the laugh, the gurgle, the crowing of the newly arrived. Laughing or crying, there is no rigid line of thought that must be obeyed or followed, but rather there is pure experience. Everything is new for a baby—it doesn't know "how to do" something; everything is an experiment. Imagine the creativity and freedom that arises from such a state of mind.

Perhaps the most persuasive teaching on this experience is recorded in the *Blue Cliff Record* when a monk asks Chao Chou,

> "Does a newborn baby have the sixth consciousnesses?"
> Chao Chou said, "Like tossing a ball on swift flowing water."
> The monk also asked T'ou Tzu, "What is the meaning of 'Tossing a ball on swift flowing water'?"
> T'ou Tzu said, "Moment to moment, nonstop flow."
> (Cleary, 437)

The question asks whether a newborn baby is conscious of hearing, seeing, touching, tasting, smelling, and thinking; it is directly asking if a person in samadhi has awareness of these six senses—are they "present." And what a response! We can almost see the ball bouncing on the flowing water. Our awareness, our minds are not dead in samadhi, but rather completely alive in T'ou Tzu's "nonstop flow."

The commentator of this collection, Yuan Wu, wrote: "A person who studies the Path must become again like an infant. Then praise and blame, success and fame, unfavorable circumstances and favorable environments—none of these can move him (Cleary, Case 80)."

Consider how a ball bounces, moves, flows over waves and under them, bumbles into eddies, and just responds exquisitely to the flow of reality around it, the reality in which it finds itself. What better image is there than a ball on swiftly flowing water? This is the flow that is the here and now—not our idea of some "enlightened" here and now, but our actual lives, genuinely lived.

To underscore this even more, the monk goes to another teacher, T'ou Tzu, and asks what Chao Chou's answer means. T'ou Tzu responds: "Moment to moment non-stop flow." Again, this story asks us to consider the quality of our samadhi as alive and responsive to the non-stop flow of life itself, to affirm being awake and ready for the shifting demands of our lives.

Isn't this the healing power of samadhi? When we can let go of our fixed ideas of reality that hold us back and fully enter the flow of our life, we encounter enjoyment, intimacy, and compassionate response. It can be gentle as a drop of dew, plain as a bowl of rice, dangerous as a whirlpool, and protective as what we can think of as the "Samadhi Family."

Samadhi, with its long history and development through so many cultures and times, resists definition, and yet, its effect on everyone who is willing to engage with it is a profound healing, a coming together of one's self as self and as the flow of time and space, of beings and non-beings. It offers us a profound healing into liberation and compassion for the world. Two women, Sona, living in Shakyamuni's time, and I, living today, share this healing power of samadhi. Surely, over time and cultural styles, our formulations and theories about how to describe it and what its benefits and hazards are will continue to change. What will remain true is the extraordinary joy and peace it offers. Freedom, with nothing left out.

How This Samadhi Is Entered: How To Sit Zazen

One master said that listening and thinking about samadhi is like being outside the gate, and zazen is returning home and sitting in peace. Zazen is a very simple practice and does not involve complicated instructions. When one studies the ancient Zen meditation manuals, it is always surprising how brief and plain they are. While speaking of the possibility of attaining the freedom and naturalness of a tiger in the mountains or a dragon in the water, the actual instructions are so concrete. Sit in a settled posture and attend to body, breath, and mind.

It is best to have a place set aside for regular zazen. Whether it is a room or just a corner, the space should be clean and uncluttered.

Ideally, place a mat or blanket on the floor and put on top of it a zafu, another type of comfortable sitting cushion, or a bench. If floor sitting is too difficult, simply use a chair.

When you do zazen, wear loose, clean clothes. At the beginning of a sitting period, it is traditional to bow to an altar, offer a stick of incense, and bow once more. Then, as you stand before your seat, bow toward and away from your cushion, bench, or chair. These acts help us to realize intention and respect. The incense is offered with the intention that this session is for all beings, for all creation, not just for oneself. The standing bow to and away from our cushion actualizes our respect for our practice and for those, whether present or not, who practice with us. The physical act of bowing, of folding our body down, placing our head in a traditionally respectful position of vulnerability, gives the ego a big break, an opportunity to let go.

When you are seated—whether cross-legged, kneeling, or in a chair—settle into the zazen posture: Place your hands on your lap or thighs, in the cosmic mudra, your right hand holding your left one, palms up, with your thumbs barely touching, forming a circle.

Do this—counting your breath, maintaining your posture, sitting still—for a thirty-minute period of zazen. Notice that the urges to move, the desire to scratch your nose, to tug on your ear, usually are ways to move away from the energies in your body. Instead of moving, stay with them, observe them, and bring your focus back to the breathing. Learn to notice how these urges fall away, only to be replaced by others, demonstrating the second noble truth: the cause of suffering is craving. All the disparate ideas, thoughts, and impulses—everything comes and goes, and yet you sit. Little by little, the chatter drops away and your body, breath, and mind are one.

Zazen is so simple. We focus on our posture and on counting our breath, and this develops samadhi, a unified mind, but the practice is not about reaching "ten." It is about training the body and mind. Let the body settle, let the breath settle, let the mind settle. Don't worry about whether your practice is working, don't judge your performance, don't tell yourself stories or find other ways to avoid this very moment. These are just ways of separating from our deepest intention and our zazen. When you do zazen, just do zazen. That's enough.

Posture

Your posture in sitting is vitally important. Sit on the forward third of your cushion or chair, so that your hips are higher than your knees, and your belly is free to move in and out without stress on your lower back. Your ears are in line with your shoulders, your head balanced gently on your neck, your eyes are slightly open, gazing down about three feet in front of you. Your chin is pointing neither up nor down, but is slightly tucked in. Place your tongue just behind your teeth on the roof of your mouth. Sway from side to side until you find your center point.

The Breath

Now attend to the breath. Breathe naturally. Breathing in, allow the breath to fully enter your body until your lower belly expands; then, breathing out, softly allow the breath to ease out through your nostrils. Notice how the breath seems to travel through the main avenues of your torso. Your belly should rise and fall naturally with each breath. Let the breath fill your lower abdomen as if it were a balloon. Later, you may notice that even the bottoms of your feet are breathing in and out. As you relax into the breath, you can begin silently counting each full cycle of breath, noting "one" on the out-breath, "two" on the next out-breath, and so on up to "ten." When you reach "ten," begin again with "one." When you realize that you have stopped counting and are caught up in thinking, simply take another breath and go back to "one."

Sit Every Day

Don't concern yourself with trying to get to some particular place or state of mind. Each day's zazen will be a little different, just like the rest of life. We practice steadiness in our daily meditation—alert, sleepy, focused—we just practice each day, through the high points and the low. When you mess up—and you will— just say, "Okay, back to my cushion." When you are sitting, you may realize that you are thinking about something else. At that moment, take a deep breath and recognize that, in that moment of realization, you have come back to now. As an old meditation manual says, as soon as you are aware of a thought, it will vanish! When we are thinking of a thing, we are lost in it, lost in thinking about "x." But when we become aware of our thinking, then we are in a secondary state. The actual thinking of "x" is gone, and there is either just awareness, or we begin a new thought based on that awareness. Either way, the original thinking is gone. If we practice daily, soon we are able to stay more often in that space of pure awareness without an object. Just breathing, just being present—we call this being naturally unified.

Zazen is a form that allows us to practice the "no form" of boundless emptiness. The freedom that is made available to us through form is one of those grand paradoxes of life. When we organize ourselves and create a structure, we also create the means to be free of structure. Form helps us by organizing and directing our energies. But we can carry our form lightly, with respect and appreciation for its gifts. Remember: this subtle discipline—settling, unifying, letting be—is called "the dharma gate of ease and joy."

Works cited

Bodhi, Bhikkhu, ed. "The Path to Liberation." *In the Buddha's Words: An Anthology of Discourses from the Pali Canon.* Somerville, MA: Wisdom, 2005.

Cleary, Thomas, trans. *The Flower Ornament Scripture: A Translation of the Avatamsaka Sutra.* Boston: Shambhala, 2014.

Cowles, Gregory. "Everybody Has Their Own English." *ArtsBeat.* The New York Times Co. 8 Dec. 2008. Web. 28 May 2016. <http://artsbeat.blogs.nytimes.com/2008/12/08/everybody-has-their-own-english/>

Dogen, Eihei. "Recommending Zazen to All People." *Beyond Thinking: A Guide to Zen Meditation.* Ed. Kazuaki Tanahashi. Boston: Shambhala, 2004.

---. "Ocean Mudra Samadhi." *Treasury of the True Dharma Eye: Zen Master Dogen's Shobo Genzo.* Ed. and trans. Kazuaki Tanahashi. 2 vols. Boston: Shambhala, 2010.

---. "On the Endeavor of the Way." Ibid.

---. "Thirty-Seven Wings of Enlightenment." Ibid.

Hallisey, Charles, trans. *Therigatha: Poems of the First Buddhist Women.* Murti Classical Library of India 3. Boston: Harvard U P, 2015.

Welwood, John. "Human Nature, Buddha Nature: Spiritual Bypassing, Relationship, and the Dharma." *John Welwood.* n.d. Web. 28 May 2016. Interview by Tina Fossella first appeared in Tricycle, Spring 2011. <http://www.johnwelwood.com/articles/TRIC_interview_uncut.pdf>

Wu, Yuan. "Case 80: Chao Chu's Newborn Baby." *The Blue Cliff Record.* Trans. Thomas and J.C. Cleary. Boston: Shambhala, 1992.

---. "Case 89: The Hands and Eyes of the Bodhisattva of Great Compassion." Ibid.

Zhengjue, Hongzhi. *Cultivating the Empty Field: The Silent Illumination of Zen Master Hongzhi.* Ed. and trans. Taigen Dan Leighton and Yi Wu. Boston: Tuttle, 2000.

Glossary

Absolute: Unconditioned, inexpressible reality; the unnameable; sometimes called the Source or the ground of all being; that which is beyond thought.

Actualize: To embody a practice; to manifest with one's life.

Avalokitesvara: Also spelled Avalokiteshvara. The bodhisattva of compassion, who may be represented as either male or female; also known as the "one who hears the cries of the world," "sound observer," Kannon, Kanzeon (Japanese), Tara (Tibetan) and Kwan-yin (Chinese). This bodhisattva's thirty-three representations, sometimes depicting many hands holding multiple implements, represent the use of the skillful methods necessary for a compassionate response to the cries of the world.

Bodhisattva: An "enlightenment being" and a helper who practices virtue, resides in the nature of compassion and wisdom, and assists other beings in the steps toward liberation. The bodhisattva promises to remain as a helper to alleviate suffering and foregoes nirvana until all beings are awakened. *Bodhisattva* can also mean a personification of Buddha Nature such as *Avalokitesvara*.

Bodhi-mind: The function of mind that is beyond dualistic consciousness; the awakened mind of wisdom that has realized the unity of subject and object and the essential empty nature of all that exists in the world of form. The awakened mind also refers to realization and insight of the four noble truths.

Buddha Nature: the true and eternal nature of all sentient life. This means that through appropriate spiritual practice all sentient life may experience the realization of enlightenment and buddhahood.

Cause and effect: See *karma*.

Dependent origination: The chain of insight that led to the Buddha's enlightenment. Following the chain backward from birth and death, the Buddha pinpointed ignorance as the ultimate cause of *dukkha*. This profound teaching requires careful study. The original words are variously translated into English. Roughly, ignorance leads to volitional action/intention, which leads to consciousness, which leads to name and form (the five skandhas), which leads to the six senses, which leads to contact, which leads to sensation, which leads to craving, which leads to grasping, which leads to becoming, which leads to birth, which leads to death. Breaking this chain at any point is liberation.

Dharma/dharmas: This word has numerous meanings depending on the context in which it is used. It can mean that which is the underlying nature of the world; the teachings or the law of universal truth; all living phenomena; the ethical rules of behavior for Buddhist practitioners; or a reflection of the content of the human mind. When capitalized, it usually refers to a Buddha's teachings.

Dukkha: Frequently translated as "suffering" or "dissatisfaction." See the Introduction for an extensive discussion of this term.

Emptiness: The Buddhist understanding that no permanent, unchanging, separate "self" can be found in any object or dharma that can be contemplated and that they, therefore, are "empty;" that the existence of any "thing," when examined with meditative wisdom and insight, is seen to be dependent on causes and conditions that are themselves empty; yet emptiness is not "void" or absence, but is ultimately the source of all existence. The Heart Sutra says: "That which is form is emptiness; that which is emptiness, form."

Fascicle: A portion of a serial document that is published separately. Dogen's *Shobogenzo*, to which this term often refers, was written over the course of his lifetime.

Five *Skandhas*, aggregates, or heaps: The means of creation for the subject/object view of reality; the name and form portion of dependent origination. The *skandhas* include form, sensation, memory (sometimes translated as "formations"), perception, and consciousness, which work together to create the view that humans call "reality."

Hinayana: Means "small vehicle" or practices focused on escaping the cycle of rebirth. Refers to the perspective of original Buddhism that is extant today in the *Theravadan* lineages.

Hindrances: Negative mental states that impede practice and lead toward unwholesome action.

Karma: The multi-dimensional universal law of cause and effect; the second link in the chain of dependent origination. The intention behind the actions of body, speech, and mind is the cause of any effect that may be experienced. By taking up the practice of the Eightfold Path, one emulates the behavior of Buddhas and bodhisattvas, and decreases the harmful operation of cause and effect in one's life. The actions of Buddhas arise from transcendental wisdom and therefore create no karma.

Koan: A paradoxical teaching, phrase, or brief narrative used in Zen training to direct the mind toward the nature of ultimate reality. A koan cannot be answered or understood through reason, but requires an insight or intuitive leap that takes one beyond logical mentation to another level of understanding.

Indra's net: A metaphor for the interdependence of all beings that originated with the *Avatamsaka Sutra*. At each joint of the net is a jewel that reflects all the other jewels in the net. In Buddhist cosmology, Indra is king of the devas (gods) that live on Mount Sumeru, the center of all worlds.

Interdependence: A core principle of Buddhism based on the teachings of dependent origination and impermanence. All phenomenal manifestations are dependent on the causes and conditions present at the moment of manifestation; none can arise in isolation.

Loving-kindness: The practice of wishing happiness to all beings. The particulars of the practice are set forth in the *Metta Sutra* or Loving-Kindness Sutra.

Lotus Sutra: A discourse of the Buddha that was delivered toward the end of his public life, said to contain the complete teachings of the Buddha. In this sutra, the Buddha is not a historical figure, but rather a transcendent Nature, which is available to everyone such that they can awaken to their own True Nature and become a Buddha themselves.

Mahayana: Literally means "great vehicle" or practices focused on awakening oneself in order to help others to awaken. See page 127 for a contrast between Hinayana and Mahayana views. The Mahayana perspective emerged around the first century CE.

Mudra: A way of holding the hands or the body in a symbolic gesture to indicate an aspect of the Buddha. All Buddhist iconography contains a particular gesture of the hands to point toward a significant aspect such as protection, care of the Sutras, supreme wisdom, concentration, fearlessness, or a myriad of other spiritual expressions.

Nirvana: Cessation (of suffering); liberation; bliss; freedom from birth and death; the original "goal" of the Eightfold Path.

Paramitas: Qualities or behaviors cultivated by bodhisattvas. They include: generosity, ethics or discipline, patience, resolute effort, meditation, and wisdom.

Precepts: Rules to live by first given by the Buddha. All stages of Buddhist ordination, from layperson to teacher, include vows to follow the precepts, which may number from 5 to as many as 311. See discussion of the Three Pure Precepts and Ten Grave Precepts on pages 83-86.

Relative: The world of forms that can be named, labeled, and objectified. Often contrasted to the absolute, the formless that cannot be named or known by thought.

Samsara: The world of suffering or dissatisfaction; the "wandering-in-circles" world as contrasted in Buddhist teaching to *nirvana*, the realm of liberation from suffering.

Sangha: The Buddhist community or the community of all beings. See discussion on page 86. One of the Three Treasures of Buddhism.

Sesshin: To "gather or collect the heart-mind." A time of intense zazen with the whole heart-mind engaged fully in practice. In a monastery, sesshin may occur several times a month lasting one week at a time. In Zen centers, sesshin may be less frequent, but the intention of full engagement of the heart-mind in zazen is the same.

Shikantaza: Shikan means "only this;" *ta* means "precisely;" *za* means "to sit." It means to forego techniques of meditation and instead, to practice what is called zazen: a state of attentive, bright awareness, and being present to everything equally without directing the mind toward any particular object.

Skandhas: See Five Skandhas.

Storehouse consciousness: A philosophical concept from the Yogacara school of Buddhism, which recognizes eight types of consciousness. Storehouse consciousness is where the traces or "seeds" of karma are stored.

Takuhatsu: The ritual practice of begging regularly undertaken by Buddhist monks to support their communities.

Three Treasures: Buddha, Dharma and Sangha or the Buddha, the teachings, and the community that practices the Buddha Way.

Zazen: Seated attentiveness in an actively present state, attentive to each passing moment, without focusing on any particular object or thought. This is also known as *shikantaza*, or just sitting, which is the practice of being one's true self, or Buddha Nature.

Zendo: A hall or room set aside for the practice of zazen. While monasteries have formal designs for the arrangement of monks and practitioners, a less formal zendo may be created in the home or office, embracing the practice of zazen in daily life.

Biographies

INTRODUCTION
Byakuren Judith Ragir

Byakuren is a senior Dharma teacher at Clouds in Water Zen Center in St. Paul, MN. She studied with Dainin Katagiri Roshi for seventeen years and received Dharma Transmission from Joen Snyder-O'Neil in the Katagiri lineage. She now writes about the dharma and makes Buddhist art quilts. See www.judithragir.org or www.cloudsinwater.org.

RIGHT VIEW
Myoan Grace Schireson

Myoan is a Zen Abbess and a clinical psychologist. She received Dharma Transmission from Sojun Mel Weitsman Roshi of the Suzuki Roshi Zen lineage. The late Fukushima Keido Roshi of Tofukuji Monastery in Kyoto, Japan, asked her to teach the koan she studied with him during her practice there. She founded two Zen practice centers and a retreat center and has empowered seven actively teaching Dharma heirs. She is the author of *Zen Women: Beyond Tea Ladies, Iron Maidens and Macho Masters* (Wisdom 2009).

RIGHT INTENTION
Zenki Mary Mocine

Zenki is the Abbess and founder of Vallejo Zen Center, Clear Water Zendo, in Vallejo, CA, which formally opened in January, 2000. She received Dharma Transmission from Sojun Mel Weitsman in 2005 at Tassajara in the Shunryu Suzuki Roshi lineage. A former attorney, Zenki began Zen practice at Berkeley Zen Center and Green Gulch Farm in 1988 and has served in various roles as senior staff at all three San Francisco Zen Center locations, including four years at Tassajara. She also leads a law dharma group for attorneys.

Right Speech
Tonen O'Connor

Tonen was ordained by Tozen Akiyama in 1994, receiving Dharma Transmission from him in 1999. She trained at the Milwaukee Zen Center and in Japan at Shogoji, Keisei Zendo, Hosshinji, and Hokyoji. Tonen served as President of the Board of the Soto Zen Buddhist Association from 2007-2009 and is currently retired after twelve years as Resident Priest at the Milwaukee Zen Center. Prior to the Zen world, Tonen worked for over forty years in the non-profit professional theater. She has two sons, four grandchildren and six great-grandchildren.

Right Action
Shodo Spring

Shodo is a Dharma heir of Shohaku Okumura, abbot of Sanshin Zen Community in Bloomington, IN. Her expression of Dharma includes "just sitting," love of the natural world, and engagement in the issues of our time, particularly climate change. Shodo's background includes a B.S. in physics, an M.S. in social work, credentials in a holistic body-work called Ortho-Bionomy, and a permaculture design certificate. Her primary profession was psychotherapy. In addition to numerous published essays, she is the author of *Take Up Your Life: Making Spirituality Work in the Real World* (Tuttle 1996). She has two children and four grandchildren.

In 2013 Shodo led the three-month Compassionate Earth Walk, a pilgrimage along the planned KXL pipeline route through the Great Plains. In 2015 she founded Mountains and Waters Alliance, humans joining with all beings to protect and restore the earth and all life. She lives and teaches in Southern Minnesota.

Right Livelihood
Misha Shungen Merrill

Misha is the founding teacher of Zen Heart Sangha in Woodside, CA, which was formed in 1996. She began practicing Zen in 1984 and received tokudo (monk ordination) in 1988. She received Dharma Transmission in 1998 from her teacher, Keido Les Kaye Roshi, the abbot of Kannon Do Zen Center and dharma heir in the lineage of Shunryu Suzuki Roshi, the founder of San Francisco Zen Center. She has practiced tea ceremony in the *Mushanokoji-senke* tradition for 30 years, teaching others for the last 10 years. Misha also teaches in a progressive elementary/middle-school in Menlo Park, CA, where she is the librarian. She resides in Woodside with her husband.

RIGHT EFFORT
Teijo Munnich

Teijo lives in Western North Carolina and is abbess of Great Tree Zen Women's temple. She also serves as Dharma teacher for Zen Center of Asheville and Charlotte Zen Meditation Society. A disciple and Dharma heir of Dainin Katagiri Roshi, Teijo studied with him from 1975 until his death in 1990. She received formal training at Hokyoji in Minnesota, Tassajara Zen Mountain Center in California and Hosshinji in Obama, Japan.

RIGHT MINDFULNESS
Hoko Karnegis

Hoko is vice-abbot at Sanshin Zen Community in Bloomington, IN and will succeed her teacher, Abbot Shohaku Okumura, when he retires. Previously she served as Communications Director at Hokyoji Zen Practice Community in southern Minnesota and as Interim Practice Director at Milwaukee Zen Center. She has spent time in several training temples in Japan, including Shogoji (Kumamoto) for the 2008 and 2011 Kokusai Angos and Toshoji Senmon Sodo (Okayama) for seven months of basic training. After completing transmission and zuise, she was appointed a *kokusaifukyoushi* (international teacher) by Sotoshu. She has a B.A. in Speech Communication/Broadcast from the University of Minnesota, and in 2009 completed an interdisciplinary master's degree there.

RIGHT SAMADHI
Pat Enkyo O'Hara

Enkyo is a Dharma successor of Bernie Glassman. She began her Zen studies with Daido Loori, and after six years, studied with Maezumi Roshi until his untimely death. She served as a Founding Teacher of the Zen Peacemaker Order, and continues to work with Bernie. In 1986 she founded the still vibrant Village Zendo, a non-residential community of Zen practitioners in Manhattan. She holds a PhD and taught for many years at New York University's Tisch School of the Arts, centering on new media technologies and social justice. Her writing has appeared in *Tricycle, Turning Wheel, Shambhala Sun, Buddhadharma* and other Buddhist journals, as well as her 2014 book, *Most Intimate, A Zen Approach to Life's Challenges*, published by Shambhala.

EDITOR
Jikyo Cheryl Wolfer

Jikyo is the Dharma heir of Eido Frances Carney, founder and abbess of Olympia Zen Center and founder of Temple Ground Press in Olympia, WA. Jikyo trained in residence at Olympia Zen Center from 1999 to 2007 with formal training at Shasta Abbey in 2006-2007. She received Dharma Transmission from Eido Roshi in 2010. Jikyo is the Dharma teacher at Joyous Refuge in Port Angeles, WA and also edited an anthology of Zen teachings, *Seeds of Virtue, Seeds of Change* (Temple Ground, 2014).

Made in the USA
San Bernardino, CA
28 August 2016